vacations
FOR THE SPIRIT

vacations
FOR THE SPIRIT

refresh and renew your life with a personal retreat

Alan Walker

BARRON'S

First edition for North America published in 2004
by Barron's Educational Series, Inc.

First published in Great Britain in 2004 by
Godsfield, a division of Octopus Publishing Group Ltd 2004

Project Editor: Sarah Doughty
Project Designer: Alison Hughes
Illustrator: Trina Dalziel
Page Makeup: Nicola Liddiard

Designed and produced for Octopus Publishing Group Ltd by
The Bridgewater Book Company

All inquiries should be addressed to:
Barron's Educational Series, Inc.
250 Wireless Boulevard
Hauppauge, New York 11788
http://www.barronseduc.com

International Standard Book Number 0-7641-2737-3
Library of Congress Catalog Card Number 2003107797

Printed and bound in China

9 8 7 6 5 4 3 2 1

Contents

Introduction

When I was a student looking for somewhere to catch up with neglected work and prepare for exams, I used to go and stay in a monastery in a quiet part of the countryside a few miles from where I lived.

The day there seemed to last a lot longer, and the distractions were far fewer than at home or college. The fixed routine and rules—for example, those about talk and silence—meant that I could get my work done and still have plenty of time left to do some reading, go for walks, rest, and just be with myself.

Over the years, I returned there many times, no longer so much with a set purpose, but simply to take a break, time out from the pressures of work and family life. I had discovered the value of what in religious language has traditionally been called a "retreat," time apart from regular activity in which we can "recharge our batteries" or reflect on where our lives seem to be going.

More recently I have come to realize how the essence of the retreat, by which I mean the self-reflection that leads to personal and spiritual growth, can be discovered in a variety of contexts and not just in the traditional

religious ones. The ancients retreated to hermitages in the desert or the mountains to discover the truth about themselves. Modern folk have a much larger range of opportunities to find fulfillment and transformation. Discovering ourselves is the greatest adventure of our lives and to begin that journey we need to rediscover what adventure means. Many people today are finding this in the kind of vacation where they do not simply relax but where they are challenged physically by the elements. Rock climbing and water rafting immediately come to mind as activities that demand the kind of concentration and determination that take us outside of our everyday selves and kindle those inner resources that we hardly knew we had.

With the packing, traveling, and change of setting, a retreat in the traditional sense closely resembles what we usually mean by a vacation. For others the journey does not need to depend on actually going away. Indeed, it is possible to take a vacation for the spirit in the very midst of daily life. Think of it as being like the "power nap" that is as effective as several hours sleep! Of course, we may be lucky enough to have the resources to spend more time away from home, but for most of us a short time out of our day can be just as valuable and effective. Furthermore, just because we are staying at home does not mean our spiritual vacation will be any less of an adventure. It can be a journey beyond our usual horizon—a time of openness to new sights, tastes, and experiences.

I like to use the word *vacation* because, outside the traditional religious world, *retreat* has a rather negative connotation. My thesaurus defines it as the opposite of *progress*, one of the most positive words in our modern vocabulary. *Retreat* implies going backward, running away, or hiding from reality—anything except being truly who, what, and where I am. For people actively engaged in spiritual development, of course, *retreat* means quite the opposite. It is closer to what we have in mind when we say going "back to basics," or getting to "the heart of the matter."

Another word used in various religious traditions is *withdrawal*. In the Christian story, Jesus withdrew into the desert to prepare for his ministry and into the garden to compose himself for his trial; and in his teaching to his disciples, he recommends that they should go into private places and shut the door behind them. In Judaism, the weekly Sabbath is a withdrawal from all work and activity, a time for rest, study, and family. In Tibetan Buddhism, life is marked by a series of withdrawals as the individual prepares for and enters the different stages of life.

Our lives are characterized by change, and there are many moments when it would be good to step back and get some perspective. It has to do with the natural movement of human growth and decline. The psychologist C. G. Jung observed that our health depends upon accepting where we are in the journey of life and living accordingly. This movement inevitably coincides with making decisions about education and employment, career development and relocation—all occasions when we might benefit from taking time out for reflection and

life assessment. In the second half of life, we turn our thoughts to death and what might follow; it would be unnatural not to do so.

There are other occasions, too, when we might feel the need to withdraw, significant times that disrupt the pattern of life and challenge our self-understanding, such as birthdays, anniversaries, and bereavements. We need a while to celebrate or to mourn before we move on.

A retreat, then, is not an escape. Rather, it is always a preparation for a return. The deepest forms of spirituality do not deny or reject the world, but encourage us to become involved in it. It is just as mistaken to reject this world in pursuit of some fanciful spiritual realm as it is to deny that life has no meaning other than material wealth and happiness. The task for all of us is to contribute to the transformation of the world through trying to create the conditions needed to bring about justice, freedom, and harmony, in the natural as well as the human realms. We make a retreat in the hope of becoming better in some small way and so furthering the greater movement toward the renewal of our environment. When we move

out of the retreat, we never quite return to the point of departure. We have moved forward, and we see the world a little differently; indeed, the world is a little different because of our effort.

So, in calling this little book *Vacations for the Spirit*, I have in mind something much more than taking a rest! The body needs rest, surely, but the spirit cries out for activity, for the spirit is that part of our being that is most alive; or rather, it is who we really are: creative, adventurous, and full of energy and resources. I offer a practical guide in which I invite you to explore how an ancient tradition can be of deep and practical benefit as we make our way in a world that often seems indifferent or even hostile to anything other than material gain and self-gratification. As we go, I will invite you to follow me through exercises and meditations to some of the routes that lead, not only to personal growth, but also to cosmic renewal.

PART 1

why take
a retreat?

WHY TAKE A SPIRITUAL VACATION?

THE OTHER DAY A CLOSE FRIEND OF MINE WAS APPLYING FOR A JOB. SHE WANTED TO TALK IT OVER WITH ME, NOT BECAUSE I KNEW ANYTHING ABOUT HER LINE OF WORK, BUT JUST BECAUSE SHE WANTED TO REFLECT AND THOUGHT I MIGHT HAVE THE TIME TO LISTEN.

We drove to an art gallery on the other side of town. The plan was to take in the exhibition quickly and then go to the gallery restaurant for lunch. Suitably inspired and relaxed, we could then concentrate on the job application. Part of me thought that this plan was typical of classic displacement activity, in which we find all sorts of things that need to be done before the task at hand can be started. Why did my friend not just sit down and fill in the form? Writers of books are, of course, very familiar with these activities. A little tidying, rearranging of the desk, another cup of coffee—and then I will turn out that chapter I promised the publisher weeks ago!

But when I myself sat down to write *this* chapter, I came to see that what we call displacement activity is not just wasting time. When we have something important—something life-changing—to accomplish, it is absurd to launch into it as if it were just the next thing on our "to do" list. We need to step back to consider both the implications of the change for the future and also how it fits in with our sense of direction and personal development.

When my friend persuaded me to go to the gallery, she was not just putting things off; she was giving me a good lesson in what is meant by vacation for the spirit.

As it happened, the exhibition that day was an installation in which visitors sat inside a circle made from audio speakers and listened to sounds recorded in a temple. Our senses were engaged in a way that took us beyond the busy life of the street outside. The meal, too—an

eclectic combination of tastes and ingredients from a variety of cultures—helped us withdraw from our regular concerns.

The exhibition turned out to be just the respite we needed before turning to that demoralizing job application—that list of qualifications and experiences beginning with the most recent, that upbeat explanation of what we might bring to and get out of the work—all to be delivered with the names of those who can vouch for us by the end of office hours tomorrow.

The spiritual life, however, has no such deadlines. It is up to us to make the time we deserve to withdraw and review our lives and decide where the spirit is leading us next. On occasion, even a few hours spent at something like an art exhibition might be enough.

THE TIMES OF YOUR LIFE

"ALL THE WORLD'S A STAGE,
AND ALL THE MEN AND WOMEN MERELY PLAYERS;
THEY HAVE THEIR EXITS AND THEIR ENTRANCES,
AND ONE MAN IN HIS TIME PLAYS MANY PARTS,
HIS ACTS BEING SEVEN AGES."

So says Shakespeare's character Jacques in *As You Like It* (Act 2, Sc.7: 139–167).

In modern times, psychologists have identified various stages of development we all go through in our personal and moral growth, but few have been able to capture the "seven ages" so powerfully as Shakespeare. We easily see ourselves in the "mewling and puking" infant; the "whining schoolboy . . . creeping like a snail unwillingly to school;" and then in that "last scene of all," "second childishness" without "teeth . . . eyes . . . taste . . ."

One of the traditional reasons for making a retreat has been to review the stages of our own lives. Spiritual writers of all traditions have recognized the importance of understanding the past for living consciously in the present and the future. The past can hold all sorts of clues about our personal journeys. Through close examination of your life so far, you may be able to identify patterns of behavior and thought of which you were not previously aware. You might discover how some past experience you had hardly considered was in fact a turning point and could still be a source of inspiration for future decision-making. Perhaps you will identify times you are ashamed of and have hidden, occasions when you hurt others or acted against what you knew was best. The retreat is a time outside of time; when you can safely explore all those incidents you have tried to forget but have never really escaped.

Chances are that you are reading this book because you have been moved inwardly to consider making a retreat. The idea—from wherever it has come—is something that touches you deeply. Try to identify when in your past you were moved in a way that led you to take the spiritual dimension of your existence seriously. In your imagination, move back through your life, through the natural stages of infancy, childhood, adolescence, young adulthood, maturity, and retirement—back from wherever you are at the present—and allow each period to present itself in a few simple words or images that characterize it in your personal history. Reflect on those images and try to accept what they are saying to you about yourself, a self that is perhaps hard to recognize. Imagine yourself at the end of life, thinking back on what it was all about and how well you did. What can you do now that will be meaningful to you then?

YOUR OWN MILESTONES

SOMETIMES WE FEEL UNEASY ABOUT OUR LIVES. WE FEEL UNHAPPY TO BE DEFINED BY OUR JOBS OR BY THE PLACES WE LIVE IN. OFTEN WE SEEM JUST TO HAVE ARRIVED WHERE WE ARE BY CHANCE, ALTHOUGH WE KNOW THAT ALL SORTS OF DECISIONS WE HAVE MADE PLAY THEIR PART, TOO.

Our real identity lies somewhere in those spaces between the circles that seem at first to define us. By taking vacations for the spirit, we create new in-between times when we can learn to make sense of the way things have worked out for us. Then we can meet the challenge of future change with more confidence and responsibility. Here are some steps for exploring your own in-between times:

Exercise

••• Sit calmly for a moment or two and let your mind drift back over your life. It will probably divide up naturally into the various places you have lived, studied, or worked. On a large sheet of paper, draw a circle for each of these periods, putting them in chronological order and writing a key word to identify each one.

••• Place the sheet in front of you and let your eye pass slowly across the circles. Move from one to the next, gently allowing yourself to linger or advance more quickly as it seems appropriate. Try to be aware of your feelings as you look upon each period of your life, but do not allow yourself to become too caught up in unhappy memories.

••• Now look at the spaces between the circles. These represent the moments of consideration, decision, and transition. What brought about the change from one stage of your life to another? Was it simply a natural development, or was it a result of some deliberate decision? Link the circles with straight lines or arrows to signify natural movement. Then use zigzags to mark times of complex decision-making. Sometimes there may be no obvious way of linking the circles because the movement was involuntary, brought on by circumstances beyond your power.

••• Select one of these in-between times for further consideration. It does not have to be one of the more difficult ones! Recall all you can about that period in your life, without struggling with your memory. Write down some words that come to mind to sum up your experience at that time. Do the same for another period, one that seems to be of a different quality. Compare the words you have used in each case to try to comprehend the hidden dynamic of your life. Ponder how you have grown, developed, and changed.

THE VALUE OF A SPIRITUAL VACATION

AS A TEENAGER, I USED TO TAKE A HALF-HOUR JOURNEY TO SCHOOL EACH DAY, WHICH IN AN UNEXPECTED WAY TOOK ON THE QUALITY OF A RETREAT. I CAN REMEMBER SITTING ALONE IN A QUIET CORNER OF THE BUS AND SUDDENLY HAVING A NEW AND TREMENDOUS SENSE OF REALITY. IT WAS AS IF AT THAT MOMENT I FIRST CAME TO REALIZE THAT I WAS TRULY ALIVE: I WAS NOT JUST PARTICIPATING IN SOME KIND OF GAME FROM WHICH I COULD EASILY WITHDRAW.

Friends have told me that they, too, have had moments when it dawned on them that life is for real and not a rehearsal. I have to say that it was not a completely happy moment. When I thought about it later, I described it to myself as the time when I realized, not only that I was alive, but also that I was nothing special.

Babies and very small children imagine themselves to be the center of the universe and have tantrums when they cannot have their own way. Older children feel their parents and teachers do not understand what they are going through, in spite of having been young once themselves.

As adults, we know that life is a series of compromises in which we hope for the best for ourselves and for our children. We say, "If only we had known then what we know now . . ." and are inclined to agree with the pundit who said, "Youth is wasted on the young." The psychoanalyst Melanie Klein said that the task of the mother is to disillusion the child. She did not mean spoil its fun, but rather help it understand that life would bring frustration and disappointment as well as happiness and satisfaction.

My thoughts often return to that moment on the bus. I think of it as the point at which I first became responsible for my life and the direction it was taking. It was the birth of conscience, if you like.

I am sure you, too, can think of a period in your life during which you moved from being dependent to being responsible—that is, the time when you grew up. For many of us, it did not happen all that long ago!

One of the greatest values of a spiritual vacation is to continue that process of disillusionment, to help each of us accept who we truly are and the responsibilities that each of us must assume. Maybe this idea makes you think twice about going on a retreat, but that is how it should be. Whatever context you choose to take your spiritual vacation, the spiritual life is not a holiday or an escape; it is always an engagement with reality.

BENEFITS
AND REWARDS

YOU HAVE BEEN TOUCHED BY THE IDEA OF TAKING A RETREAT. ACCEPT THAT THIS DISCOVERY IS MORE THAN JUST HEARING ABOUT AN INTERESTING NEW PLACE TO VISIT. CONSIDER CAREFULLY HOW YOU CAME TO HEAR ABOUT THE IDEA AND BE THANKFUL FOR WHOEVER BROUGHT IT TO YOUR ATTENTION.

- What are your present circumstances?
- Are you in a time of change or decision-making?
- What, or who, is currently making a claim on you?
- Do you feel in need of guidance or of an opportunity to reflect?

Spiritual possibilities do not present themselves to us accidentally. They are central to our lives and well-being. It is up to us to recognize this truth and identify them as gifts.

Exercise

••• Reflect back on the major events of your life, paying attention to the times of transition. Are there things you would change? Are there pieces of unfinished business that continue to haunt you?

••• Now think yourself forward. Imagine you are floating into the future on a magic carpet. You can see some of the possibilities and opportunities, but you are not yet caught up in them. There are whole areas covered in cloud that you cannot see. How does the future feel to you at this moment? Do you go forward with apprehension or with optimism and a sense of a quest?

••• In what ways do your feelings about the past and present affect your hopes for the future? Do you have a sense of wanting to make up for the past or to escape your world as it is?

••• Now recall or imagine a happy holiday.

••• To begin with, you probably needed time to relax and put aside some of the concerns you brought with you from your job or domestic life: Will they cope without you, or just create more work for your return? Toward the end of your break, these worries probably started to come back, and it became harder to relax. But in the middle—for a few days or for that week—you did find some rest.

••• Accept that the invitation to the retreat will have a similar structure. It will not necessarily be a time of perfect peace, but it includes that possibility, if you are willing to prepare for it.

SETTING PERSONAL GOALS

WHAT DO YOU MOST DESIRE? OBVIOUSLY, IT WOULD BE EASY FOR YOU TO MAKE A LIST OF ALL THE THINGS YOU WOULD LIKE TO DO OR OWN. BUT I DO NOT THINK YOU WOULD HAVE BEEN DRAWN TO THIS BOOK FOR THE PURPOSE OF FULFILLING AMBITIONS AND INCREASING WEALTH AND POSSESSIONS. RATHER, YOU ARE HERE BECAUSE YOU WANT TO STEP BACK SOMEWHAT TO REFLECT ON THE MEANING OF DEEPER GOALS AND BENEFITS.

A vacation is rarely the time when you advance a career or improve your finances. You know it is more likely to do the opposite, but you are prepared at least to consider taking the risk. And you know, too, that a spiritual vacation is likely to raise all sorts of questions about the real value of so much of what we think we long for.

If you were to make a list of the things you most desire, I am sure you would probably begin with the well-being of those close to you and with better health and conditions for people generally. Next, you might be particularly concerned for the natural world and the environment. Finally, in the appropriate order, you might follow the wish to preserve the outstanding achievements of human culture, along with examples of humbler feats.

No one would criticize such worthy goals. But the call to make a retreat is asking us something more precise: What do I truly desire? Have I really placed these objectives on my personal agenda? Am I living my life in a way that might bring them closer? In short, how truly engaged am I with what I think is right?

When I ask myself if I am genuinely oriented toward increasing the amount of good in the world, and actually engaged in the project, I feel thrown into confusion. I know I do truly wish for the best, but I hardly know how to do anything about it.

The goal of every retreat is that I should come to desire that which is best for me. I should come to see that what is best for me is that I discover my place in the world and its spiritual destiny. It sounds like an extraordinary wish, but really all that is being asked is that each of us be shown how to fit into the bigger picture, how we might each act in a way that resonates with the will of God. Beyond our apparent differences, our personal goals are actually identical: we all want to know how to live meaningfully.

WHAT DO I HOPE TO ACHIEVE?

MANY OF US NOWADAYS HAVE THE OPPORTUNITY TO TAKE TIME OUT AT DIFFERENT STAGES IN OUR LIVES. YOUNG PEOPLE MAY COMPETE WITH EACH OTHER TO DISCOVER THE MOST EXOTIC PLACE TO EXPLORE OR THE MOST UNUSUAL PURSUIT TO ENGAGE IN BEFORE GOING TO COLLEGE. MANY SEIZE THE OPPORTUNITY A FEW MONTHS AFTER GRADUATING, BELIEVING THAT THIS PERIOD MIGHT BE THE LAST CHANCE TO DO SOMETHING INTERESTING AND DIFFERENT BEFORE ENTERING THE WORLD OF EMPLOYMENT. OLDER PEOPLE MAY HAVE DISCOVERED THAT WE DO NOT NECESSARILY KEEP THE SAME CAREER FOR OUR ENTIRE LIFE AND MAY FIND OURSELVES MAKING BIG CHANGES AS WE MOVE TO FIND DIFFERENT EMPLOYMENT OR RETRAIN FOR A NEW OCCUPATION.

At times like this taking time out can be a helpful way of preparing for what is to come and also for coming to terms with what has gone before. However much we might regret the past it has brought us to where we are now and the new possibilities and opportunities that lie ahead. Many people find that their personal "system"—physically, emotionally, intellectually—needs a good shake out and the best

way of doing this is through some challenging activity. "Survival" experiences, overland treks, river journeys, jungle and mountain expeditions are possibilities now for far more people than professional explorers. But any kind of "adventure" that calls for awakening inner strengths, developing basic skills, cooperating with others can help us prepare for the next stage of our journey.

Experienced travelers to foreign places know that adventure and interest depend on preparation. You are far more likely to have genuine encounters with local people if you take the trouble to learn a bit of the local language and to familiarize yourself with the customs and prevailing political and social situations.

At the same time, you need to be open to discovering the new. You need to consider the possibility that the guidebook might be wrong and that a true encounter depends upon having your ideas and preconceptions challenged.

Exercise

••• As you prepare for your retreat, ask yourself what you hope to achieve, and write down the concerns that have brought you to this stage. Then put the list to one side just out of reading range.

••• Open your thoughts to the other things that matter to you at the present time, and make a note of them.

••• Then put the two lists next to each other. Which of the items are really important?

••• The spirit moves in mysterious ways, but it rarely does so without leaving clues. Look for these as you prepare for your retreat, and open yourself to the new possibilities that await you.

PART 2

retreat basics

PLANNING YOUR RETREAT

FOR MANY YEARS, I WAS FORTUNATE TO HAVE THE USE OF A FRIEND'S HOUSE IN SWITZERLAND IN THE SUMMER. IT WAS ON A HILLSIDE OVERLOOKING A LAKE, A FEW MINUTES WALK OUTSIDE A PICTURE-POSTCARD VILLAGE. IN SHORT, IT WAS PERFECT, AND I ALWAYS LOOKED FORWARD TO GOING BACK. FOR SOME YEARS, HOWEVER, THE TIMING WAS NOT RIGHT FOR MY FRIEND OR FOR ME, AND I WENT ELSEWHERE.

Elsewhere, however, often proved a disappointment, an experience most of us have probably had on holiday. We have booked some place from reading about it or seeing it illustrated in a brochure, only to discover that the reality does not quite meet our expectations. If only we could have paid a brief visit before committing ourselves, as we would have done with practically every other relocation of home, school, or work. Just because a vacation only lasts a short time it still represents a great investment of hope and expectation. If it disappoints, we know we might have a long time to wait before we have another opportunity for time out.

And even though a vacation for the spirit might be for only a day or two, it can represent an enormous investment of personal time and energy. I believe that once you have had the experience of making a retreat, you will want to do so again and again; but, as with any other endeavor, the hardest thing is starting.

Even before you think about where you might go on retreat or how you might plan one yourself, it is worth getting a feel for some of the traditional elements. Actually, there is nothing that mysterious or esoteric about a retreat. What matters is not so much what you do as the deliberate attention you give to it.

What might be new to you is simply setting at least a day aside for inward thinking. It has to be at least a day, I think; otherwise, we are not talking "retreat," but "quiet time" or "session." The basic elements of a retreat are sleeping, eating, resting, and whatever is appropriate to call the spiritual activities of prayer, meditation, and devotion—I rather like the word *sitting* used in the Zen tradition. To these essentials should be added, in many instances, guidance or spiritual direction, and, in all cases, a period for reflecting on what has happened and how it will affect your ordinary life. Some of these elements you will probably already have experienced, but you might like to sample the others.

SAMPLING THE RETREAT

BEFORE GOING ON A RETREAT IT IS A GOOD IDEA TO PREPARE YOURSELF MENTALLY FOR THE EXPERIENCE—HERE ARE SOME PRACTICAL SUGGESTIONS.

Sleeping ••• Before going to bed, consider your plan to experiment with being on retreat the following day. Affirm your resolve to spend time sitting in contemplation, to savor thankfully the food that energizes you, and to enjoy the time you will have for rest. Prepare your space for the morning by removing from sight the clutter of the day and putting aside unfinished work. Make sure the space is clear and straightened. Place there some symbolic object, such as a stone, a flower, or a devotional picture, so that you will recall immediately upon wakening that you have special plans for the day.

Sitting ••• Try to sit quietly and comfortably for short periods. Try just a minute to begin with, then perhaps five and ten. Concentrate on the sounds you can hear, first in the room and then outside. How many separate sounds are there? How many are natural, such as birdsong, and how many are human made, such as traffic noise or a ticking clock? Come gently out of the silence, and then try to recall the experience briefly. Jot down a couple of words that describe the experience in a notebook.

Eating ••• Prepare your table beautifully with flowers and well-arranged dishes and cutlery, as if you were entertaining a very special guest. Instead of taking food straight from the pan, use serving bowls! Pause for a moment before starting your meal to appreciate all that is before you—how each individual item has its own texture, color, and taste. Give thanks as well for those whose labor produced this food and brought it to you. Pause again between each mouthful and course to savor your meal fully; and at the end of it, reflect on your good fortune in having all you need in a world of injustice and inequality.

Resting ••• Recall a time when you were without cares or worries, when you began each day enthusiastically and open to what it might bring. Focus on some of the images that come to mind as you do so, and try to see if something similar is on your present horizon. Maybe there is a garden you could visit, or a particular walk you could take to recapture some of the feelings you remember. Withdraw to some place where you cannot be disturbed, if only for half an hour. Say to yourself, "this is my time." Turn off your mobile phone. Make sure nothing is allowed to intrude on this special interlude. Afterward, consider how this time apart felt to you, and record it in a few words in your notebook.

THE RIGHT PLACE

THE WORD *RETREAT* SUGGESTS MOVEMENT AND REMINDS US THAT THE SPIRITUAL LIFE IS A JOURNEY RATHER THAN A PLACE. FOR SOME PEOPLE THE JOURNEY WILL BE A LITERAL ONE TO A COMMUNITY OR CENTER ASSOCIATED WITH A PARTICULAR TEACHER OR MOVEMENT. ACKNOWLEGED SPIRITUAL TEACHERS FREQUENTLY LEAD CONFERENCES OR TRAINING SESSIONS THAT ATTRACT SEEKERS FROM NEAR AND FAR. BUT SIMPLY ATTENDING A MEETING OR LECTURE DOES NOT CONSTITUTE MAKING A RETREAT, ANYMORE THAN VISITING A CHURCH OR TEMPLE CONSTITUTES A DEVOTIONAL EXERCISE.

To take a retreat is to make a decision and to endeavor to carry it through. This decision has to do with trying to get in touch with your inner life to see how it relates to your everyday outer life and striving to bring the two into greater harmony. Essentially, that effort—together with the recognition that we relate to a higher reality with our whole being—is all that is meant by the word *spirituality*. We are not spiritual beings because we have an inner life; nor does being spiritual involve denying the material. Rather, we become spiritual by bringing the two together into harmony with the third: divine reality. No wonder the number "three" plays such a powerful part in the traditions!

So first, when it comes to choosing the right place for your retreat, ask yourself if perhaps you are already there. If you feel the need to go away from your familiar surroundings, it might be because you are seeking to escape, not go on retreat. Of course, a busy household is unlikely to be conducive to prayer and meditation, but, as you prepare to go elsewhere, try to ensure that you are leaving a peaceful home behind. If your partner or family resents your going away, or relationships at home are not harmonious, you are likely to find it impossible to focus seriously on anything else.

Secondly, do not think you are going to find the right place immediately. Explore the possibilities. Perhaps you are lucky enough to have a place in your home—even a spare room—that you can turn into your quiet space. There may be a church nearby that is open outside of service times, or a shelter in a garden or park that feels right for you. If you are aware of a religious house of some kind—a convent, monastery, or meditation center—inquire if you can visit for a day or stay overnight. Try them all out. Some people prefer to be close to, but not part of, a tradition by renting space in a guest house or small hotel near an acknowledged sacred site. The important thing is that your location or situation is conducive to your spiritual desire and does not interfere with it.

EXPLORING RETREAT CENTERS

YOU MAY FEEL A LITTLE APPREHENSIVE ABOUT VISITING A RETREAT CENTER, COMMUNITY, OR RELIGIOUS HOUSE FOR THE FIRST TIME, BUT I ENCOURAGE YOU TO PUT ANY MISGIVINGS ASIDE. MANY PLACES OFFER READY-MADE RETREATS, PROVIDING AN OASIS FROM THE OUTSIDE WORLD. SOME PROVIDE ACTIVITIES, WORKSHOPS, AND FACILITIES FOR LEARNING, WHILE OTHERS PROVIDE QUIET DAYS DIRECTED AT PARTICULAR GROUPS OR WITH A THEME. IF THESE DO NOT APPEAL, ASK IF YOU CAN JUST HAVE A QUIET DAY OR DAYS THERE. MOST HOUSES OFFER THIS KIND OF HOSPITALITY, SOME FOR A SET CHARGE, OTHERS FOR A SUGGESTED DONATION.

A telephone call or written request for a brochure is the place to start. The brochure will explain the identity and mission of the center and probably give some indication of the structure of the day: the times of meals and services, in particular. Christian and Buddhist centers, which are the most common, will probably have short periods of prayer or meditation throughout the day, from early morning until the last thing at night (which will likely be a bit earlier than you are used to). These sessions are usually optional, but you will want to attend most at least once to get a feel for the place. Many will offer the services of a spiritual guide or teacher, sometimes called a "director." Sometimes these services are central to the life of the house, so you may want to begin somewhere less structured. Do not expect to find the place that suits you immediately; on the other hand, do not think you must go somewhere exotic or distant to discover what you are seeking.

Most centers will be happy to welcome you for a short visit and will arrange for you to speak to a member or "guest master." They will not be surprised nowadays to learn that you may not belong to or even have much knowledge of their tradition. It is more than likely that many of the members began as seekers like yourself— which is a gentle warning that some centers, particularly those belonging to newly founded movements, are bound to have recruitment in mind.

I have always found that, when visiting a place for the first time, I want to learn a little about its history. You may wish to do the same. It is useful to explore the building and the garden, if there is one, as well as the wider location and the neighborhood. The purpose is to assess the place, not in a judgmental sense, but just to see if it feels right for you. Above all, you want to find out if you can be quiet there, or if there are things that do not allow you to be at ease.

CREATING A RETREAT SPACE OF YOUR OWN

YOU MAY WANT TO CREATE A RETREAT SPACE OF YOUR OWN AS AN OCCASIONAL ALTERNATIVE TO GOING AWAY OR BECAUSE YOU HAVE NOT BEEN ABLE TO FIND A SUITABLE CENTER NEARBY. IT COULD BE A ROOM OR PART OF A ROOM IN YOUR HOUSE, A PLACE IN THE GARDEN, OR EVEN A GARDEN ITSELF.

Most guides suggest that prayer or meditation space should be simple and rather empty. Rooms in retreat houses are usually pretty bare, containing just a bed, dresser, table and chair, and some symbol or image of the host tradition, such as a cross or picture. But this does not mean that a place of your own has to be similar. Indeed, I hesitate to say *what* it should be like, because what matters is that it is conducive to your own needs. Clearly, you do not want the space to be so full of distractions that you cannot find inner stillness, but what suits each person best is an individual matter. I am always struck by how the rooms of the spiritual fathers in the Eastern Christian Church always seem to be full of color and texture in comparison to the starkness of those of their Western counterparts. The same is true of the different traditions of Buddhism: the Hinayana tradition of the south is simple and plain in its taste, whereas that of Tibet and the north is rich and intense.

Exercise

••• As you are making your own space, you are completely free to experiment with contents and furnishings. But it is best to bear in mind the idea of the retreat as a movement and so think in terms of the essentials you would need for a journey. Do not take more (or less) than you need. Try not to take things that you would miss if you lost or gave them away en route. And try to create a slight sense of unfamiliarity or dislocation to remind you that you are

traveling. I have a large picture of an ancient stone circle in my space, which always evokes in me a sense of adventure and mystery and takes me quickly beyond my daily cares.

••• Remember also that, as a retreat is about movement, your personal space could be something you simply imagine. That is to say, your imagined retreat could be a walk or a place in a park, the countryside, or even the town.

MAKING TIME IN YOUR BUSY LIFE

PLANNING TIME AWAY CAN BE DIFFICULT, BUT A FEW SIMPLE CHARTS CAN HELP YOU CREATE YOUR OWN RETREAT SCHEDULE.

Exercise

••• To begin with, think about how you normally fill your day. On a large sheet of paper, write down your typical schedule as a chart, from the first thing you do in the morning to the last thing you do at night. Calculate and make a note of how long you spend on particular activities, and put these alongside the timings on your sheet.

••• Now pause for a moment and ask yourself why you chose this kind of day. Most of us have three kinds of days in our regular lives: the working day, the weekly day off, and the holiday. You probably chose a working day to illustrate what is "normal," and of course there are, regrettably, more of them than the other kinds.

••• Now produce a chart showing how you might spend weekly days off and holidays.

••• When you think of the retreat, which sort of day do you imagine it to be? Is it work or is it a vacation?

••• Now think about how you would like your day to be, and write that down. No one is going to see it, so it does not matter if you would rather not get up before the afternoon! Your day off probably resembles this schedule, especially if you live alone or do not have any responsibility for others. But try to write down what you would really like, regardless of how you have to fit it in with unexpected phone calls and shopping hours. You probably know already whether you are a morning or an evening sort of person—whether you

function best late at night, in the early hours, or at some other time. Now that we live in a twenty-four-hour society, we are less constrained to operate in any typical kind of way. In short, you no longer need to feel guilty about the hours you keep, nor obliged to believe in the wisdom of the ancients that early is best.

••• Now throw those charts away and make your own retreat schedule, one that works for you. Do not force yourself to conform to some preconceived idea of what a retreat should be like, but always aim for balance. Give yourself time for eating, sleeping, resting, and appropriate work. Many people find that having some small practical activity helps them relax: minor clothing repairs, a jigsaw puzzle, a piece of modeling clay. Do not be afraid to change your routine if you find it is not working.

CREATING A SCHEDULE THAT WORKS FOR YOU

A typical retreat house timetable:

(Only start times are listed.)

MORNING

7:30 A.M.	Morning worship
8:00 A.M.	Breakfast
10:00 A.M.	Talk or meeting
10:30 A.M.	Private meditation

AFTERNOON/EVENING

12:15 P.M.	Midday worship
1:00 P.M.	Lunch
2:00 P.M.	Free time
4:30 P.M.	Talk or meeting
5:00 P.M.	Private meditation
6:30 P.M.	Evening worship
7:00 P.M.	Supper
8:15 P.M.	Talk or meeting
9:30 P.M.	Night worship

A personal schedule:

(Only start times are listed.)

MORNING

8:15 A.M.	Silence
8:30 A.M.	Breakfast
9:30 A.M.	Spiritual reading or devotion
10:00 A.M.	Meditation
11:00 A.M.	Break
11:30 A.M.	Meditation

AFTERNOON/EVENING

12:15 P.M.	Preparation of meals/cleaning
1:00 P.M.	Lunch
2:00 P.M.	Rest/walk
5:00 P.M.	Spiritual reading or devotion
6:00 P.M.	Preparation of meals/cleaning
7:00 P.M.	Supper
8:15 P.M.	Review of day/preparation for next day
9:00 P.M.	End-of-day devotion

THE RIGHT GUIDANCE

TWO YOUNG MEN ARE HURRYING AWAY FROM A CITY WHERE A FRIEND, ANOTHER YOUTH, HAS JUST MET A VIOLENT DEATH. THEY ARE GRIEF-STRICKEN AND IN SHOCK. UNABLE TO COMPREHEND WHAT HAS HAPPENED AND FEARFUL FOR THEIR OWN SAFETY, THEY HAVE DECIDED TO RUN AWAY, JUST AS ANY OF US MIGHT DO WHEN CONFRONTED WITH PAIN AND CONFUSION. THEY GO OVER THE INCIDENT AGAIN AND AGAIN IN THEIR OWN MINDS AND IN THEIR FRANTIC CONVERSATION.

Suddenly, they are joined by a mysterious stranger, who asks what is upsetting them. The men come to a stop in astonishment that someone might not share their troubles, but the stranger proves a good listener. He allows them to tell their story and express their feelings without interruption, and then he interprets it for them so that they begin to see the meaning of the terrible event they have witnessed. So helpful is this stranger that when he tries to move on, they plead with him to stay. After spending further time and sharing a meal with him, the two men resolve to abandon their flight and return to the city. Their earlier decision to run away now seems misguided.

Christians will recognize the story of the encounter of the disciples with the risen Jesus on the road to Emmaus. It is also one of the classic texts on spiritual direction or guidance. The stranger is a model guide who walks alongside the men without imposing his presence on them. He listens more than he speaks. He empathizes with them, taking their pain seriously, but shows how it can have an inner meaning that is greater than the hurt it inflicts.

It is important, however, not to dwell too much on the suffering of the individuals in the story. The point is that they have come to a crisis in their spiritual lives and do not know which way to turn. The stranger gently helps them discover that way for themselves.

The word *crisis*, rather than suggesting some kind of disaster, originally referred to the need to make a judgment concerning, for example, taking one course of action or another. The decision to take our spiritual lives seriously is a kind of crisis, in that sense, and one for which we might feel the need for guidance. Of course, the principal guide is the spirit itself, acting upon us and acting within us; but at some stage, we might want to have a "stranger" to speak with.

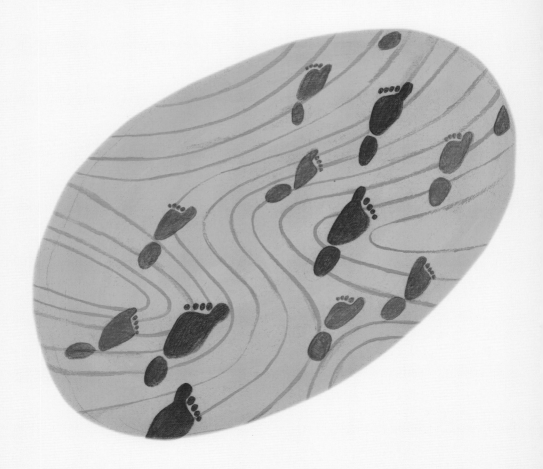

CHOOSING A SPIRITUAL GUIDE

IN THE CHRISTIAN TRADITION, SOME RETREATS ARE CALLED "INDIVIDUALLY GUIDED," AS PARTICIPANTS ARE ALLOCATED A DIRECTOR FOR THE TIME OF THEIR STAY. MANY DIRECTORS PREFER TO BE KNOWN AS "COMPANIONS," OR EVEN JUST BY THEIR PERSONAL NAMES, TO EMPHASIZE THAT THEY ARE NOT PRESCRIBING A PROGRAM TO BE FOLLOWED BUT ARE THERE TO HELP THE INDIVIDUAL HEAR THE CALL OF THE SPIRIT AND RESPOND ACCORDINGLY.

In another sort of retreat, the group attends talks in which topics are suggested for meditation. These talks are often on a particular theme that has been advertised beforehand. Although private meetings with the speaker may be arranged, they are not integral to the retreat and amount more to general spiritual advice or discussion rather than to the kind of guidance that depends on a closer relationship.

In other spiritual traditions—such as Buddhism, for instance—terms such as "teacher" or "master" are often used, partly because there is no other way to translate what would otherwise be unfamiliar terms into English. What is often lost in the translation is the importance of the relationship between the teacher and the pupil. And since Eastern traditions are relatively new in the West, there may be an emphasis on teaching here that would not be so necessary in the original culture.

Try to be clear in your mind about what you are looking for in a spiritual mentor. How prepared are you to share deeply personal information about yourself? How confident are you that the guide will respect your disclosures? Will he or she observe a rule of strict confidentiality?

Many traditions share a strong conviction that when the pupil is ready, the teacher will appear. The pupil might search for a teacher, but the teacher will never promote himself or herself. A spiritual guide, in a similar fashion, is not someone who has set out to take on the role, but one who has come to be accepted and recommended as such. Genuine spiritual guides see themselves as conversational partners who have much to learn as well as to teach.

So exercise care in seeking a spiritual guide. Ask for suggestions from other members of your community, or spend time listening to several teachers before approaching them. Be patient. Remember, also, that you can always change your mind.

An authentic guide will always agree to an initial meeting to determine if you are right for each other and not expect an agreement to follow inevitably. Should you decide to work together, you should make sure that there is clarity about commitment to meeting times and places and especially about any kind of payment or donation.

DIRECTING YOUR OWN RETREAT

MANY TRADITIONS STRONGLY ASSERT THAT NO ONE CAN DIRECT HIMSELF OR HERSELF SPIRITUALLY; AN EXPERIENCED GUIDE IS ALWAYS NEEDED. GIVEN THIS BELIEF, IT IS SURPRISING THAT SOME OF THE PRINCIPAL WRITINGS RECOMMEND PEOPLE WHO HAVE TAKEN RETREATS TO BEGIN LEADING THEM FOR OTHERS BEFORE HAVING GAINED MUCH EXPERIENCE.

The explanation is that the "knowledge" the guide possesses to pass on to the one on retreat is that they are both fellow travelers on the same path. This knowledge, rather than concerning a body of esoteric teachings, has to do with a lived experience to be treasured and shared. As soon as you have tasted the flavor of the divine, you will feel compelled to communicate it to others. But before that, you will want to savor it for yourself.

This is how a self-directed retreat is best understood. You are not being asked to explore some place on your own and for the first time, but rather to compile a map of somewhere you have already visited.

It may be only a sketchy map at first, but it will immediately be of value to those who have never made the journey. Over time, you will be able to fill in some of the detail, and it will become more and more valuable. You will be able to compare your map with that of others, both those who have gone before you and those who have set out with your directions as their guide. You may not feel you have advanced very far down the spiritual path, but do not lose confidence. Always remember that spiritual growth is a gift, not an achievement.

Begin, then, by looking for the traces of the sacred in your life. Set aside twenty minutes to review your spiritual adventure.

Exercise

••• Think through your life by allowing the memories of the different periods to pass through your mind. Begin with your infancy and the time of early childhood before you went to school. Recall gratefully the care and nurturing you received from your parents.

••• Try to remember the earliest times you spent alone. Were these times pleasant or frightening?

••• Was it in this period that you first began to sense a greater reality touching your life? If this is the case, try to stay with the memories and images evoked.

••• When you feel ready, return to the present moment, and use your journal to record your experience in words and images.

••• Repeat the exercise until you record experiences in your life up to the present.

the spiritual retreat

THE BENEFITS OF A SPIRITUAL RETREAT

NO ONE REALLY CHOOSES TO MAKE A RETREAT AS THEY WOULD CHOOSE TO GO SHOPPING OR TO THE MOVIES. YOUR SPIRIT DRAWS YOU TO THE RETREAT, JUST AS YOUR BODY CALLS OUT TO YOU FOR REST. THE DIFFERENCE IS THAT YOUR BODY IS DESTINED TO DECLINE AND DISINTEGRATE—AS FATIGUE AND EXHAUSTION CONSTANTLY SERVE TO REMIND US. HOWEVER, WHEREAS THE SPIRIT CARRIES THE PROMISE OF ETERNITY, THE SPIRIT IN US LONGS TO GROW AND FILL US. BUT THE SPIRIT IS CONSTANTLY FRUSTRATED BY OUR OBSESSION WITH MUNDANE AFFAIRS AND OUR MISTAKEN BELIEF THAT THEY ARE OUR TRUE CALLING.

The great spiritual traditions of the world all recognize some identity or deep relationship between the individual human spirit and the divine. It is a relationship, however, in which the divine is the "senior partner," who takes the initiative, constantly drawing us toward what is greater than ourselves. This relationship might be of a greater reality attracting its lesser manifestations back to itself—as in the Hindu and Buddhist image of the great ocean drawing in the dewdrop—or of an individual God seeking to bring his creation into the deepest possible personal relationship with himself, as in the Abrahamic traditions. The difference that separates us from the divine is that we are inhabitants of time and not yet of eternity. It is with time, then, that the spirit works as it seeks to give us a taste of the transcendent. The call to retreat is nothing less than an invitation to glimpse heaven in the ordinary.

No doubt many people who go on a retreat hope that the benefits of their time-out will occur in the more immediate future. Certainly, a retreat promises rest and opportunities to read, think, and prepare for change or decision-making; but what distinguishes it from a mere holiday is that, however much we concentrate on this or that activity, there is actually something else going on. We are being shaped, tuned, brought into harmony with a power greater than our own or any other on earth. Furthermore, our small concerns are not devalued but are caught up in the divine plan for the world and shown to be potential instruments of power.

What makes a retreat truly spiritual is that we enter it with a sense of openness to the future—or, if you prefer, to the divine will. Expect to be changed, if only in some tiny way. Accept that the retreat itself is a great gift.

PREPARING TO ENTER A RETREAT

PREPARE TO ENTER THE RETREAT WITH A SENSE OF AWE. WHAT YOU ARE ABOUT TO DO IS NOT ONLY FOR YOURSELF BUT ALSO FOR THE WORLD! THE OPPORTUNITY BEING GIVEN TO YOU IS TO TAKE PART IN THE REORDERING OF THE WORLD IN ACCORDANCE WITH THE WAY OF THE SPIRIT, RATHER THAN IN THE WAY OF DECAY AND OBLIVION CHARACTERISTIC OF PHYSICAL REALITY. BUT DO NOT BE PUT OFF BY THE MAGNITUDE OF RESPONSIBILITY ON YOUR SHOULDERS! YOUR PART, ALTHOUGH VITAL, MAY BE ONLY A SMALL ONE. THE TRANSFORMATION OF THE UNIVERSE BEGINS WITH TINY ADJUSTMENTS. THINK OF HOW TINY THE ADJUSTMENTS ARE THAT THE CLOCKMAKER OR PIANO TUNER MAKES TO HIS INSTRUMENT, AND YET HOW USELESS IT IS WITHOUT THEM.

So, as you get ready to go away or to enter the space you have created for your retreat, recognize that all your small preparations have some bearing on what is to come. You want the retreat to be a time of close awareness, so try to make sure that your outside reality will not impinge—either literally, as colleagues try to contact you, or psychologically, as your thoughts wander to unfinished business. The same, of course, goes for personal and social matters. A retreat is about taking responsibility for yourself, and that work must be underway before you begin.

Many first-timers worry about what to take with them or what they should wear at a retreat center. These fears are not trivial. They are deep concerns about what we need to face the spirit and in what light we will appear. The answer to the first concern is "very little," and to the latter, "it does not matter." But maybe such assurances at this point do not help, and we will look at the more practical details later.

As the retreat is a gift of time, the best way you can prepare for it is to give it time in return. You will probably have arranged to take your retreat some weeks in advance. Use that time to reflect on the decision you have made and to make sure that all the practical arrangements are in place, so that you do not take everyday concerns with you. Practice being on your own for short periods; get used to having your telephone turned off; spend some time reflecting on the direction of your life and how you see your future. In short, begin tuning in to the call of the spirit who is inviting you to be a guest.

A PRE-RETREAT CHECKLIST

AS MENTIONED BEFORE, MAKE SURE YOU HAVE MADE ALL THE PRACTICAL ARRANGEMENTS FOR BEING AWAY, AS YOU WOULD FOR ANY ABSENCE FROM HOME. IN PARTICULAR, AND BECAUSE IT IS IN KEEPING WITH THE SPIRIT OF THE RETREAT, ENSURE THAT EVERYONE WHO MIGHT BE EXPECTING TO HEAR FROM YOU KNOWS YOU WILL BE GONE AND IS CONFIDENT YOU WILL BE IN TOUCH ON YOUR RETURN.

Exercise

••• Because you are going as a guest to the retreat, you should let your hosts know of any special needs or requirements you might have—for example, diet or mobility. Check that you have read the information sheets about what they provide such as towels and soap and so on, and what you are expected to bring for yourself. Retreat houses are simple places, and you might still want to bring your own supplies, not to create luxury, but just so that you are not irritated by their absence or your forgetfulness.

••• Read up on the location to get a sense of what the weather might be like, and take practical clothing and footwear with you.

••• Take a few objects or pictures to help you feel at home in your room. The retreat is not an abandoning of life or any kind of symbolic rejection of the world, so there is every reason to take something to remind you of your usual surroundings and your happy intention to return to them. Such items are far more valuable than token "holy" ones bought especially for the occasion.

••• Most guides usually recommend that you do not take books with you, other than perhaps the sacred text of your tradition, on which

you may be invited to meditate. Some people—including myself—are terrified by the idea of being stuck somewhere with nothing to read, so give careful consideration to your choice. It is important not to take something that will distract you from your real intention, so poetry, for instance, might be preferred to a novel. There is something to be said for taking a spiritual book from another tradition, which might gently challenge some of your preconceived ideas about the movement of the spirit and how you should live. I hope you might dip into such a book, but only to send you back to the real business of your retreat.

••• The only book you *must* take, however, is a notebook to serve as your retreat journal.

KEEPING A RETREAT JOURNAL

A NOTEBOOK IS A POWERFUL SPIRITUAL TOOL. YOUR NOTEBOOK DESERVES TO BE SELECTED CAREFULLY AND TREATED WELL. IT WILL PROBABLY BE HARD RATHER THAN SOFT BOUND, LARGE RATHER THAN SMALL, AND PLAIN OR FAINTLY, RATHER THAN BOLDLY, LINED. THE PURPOSE OF THE NOTEBOOK IS TO HELP YOU CONVERSE WITH THE SPIRIT, SO IT COMMANDS CARE AND RESPECT WHILE IN USE AND IN STORAGE. KEEP IT WITH YOU THROUGHOUT YOUR RETREAT, OR TURN TO IT QUICKLY UPON FINISHING ANY PARTICULAR TASK OR ACTIVITY.

Exercise

••• Jot down whatever strikes you in just the way it strikes you. It could be a word, a phrase, or an idea, or it could be a view or a sensation. Record such gifts as briefly and concisely as possible, so that you will be able to recall them almost completely in the future. A retreat is like peeling away paint on a window; the light shines through with different strengths in seemingly random places.

••• Make notes of guidance you receive in groups or individually. But do not try to record everything the moment you hear it, as you would in a classroom or at a lecture. It is best to do so afterward, because what you remember after the fact is probably what is meant for you.

••• Use your notebook as a journal to reflect on, rather than just to record what happened each day. It does not really matter what you had for breakfast, unless it moved you to some specific thought or feeling. Always pay attention to things that seem odd or out of place and to particular experiences of comfort and calm or of unhappiness and sadness.

••• The entries in your diaries do not need to be in words. Some people express themselves far better in pictures or symbols. And even if you think you have little talent, trying a different medium to express something that has moved you can be very rewarding.

••• Most importantly, the book is a tool and not just a repository for dead ideas. At the end of each day, spend a few minutes to look through it and add new responses and reactions. Try to read it closely, as if the language were unfamiliar or you were decoding a secret message. Listen for the "Word" behind the words that is speaking to you alone.

WHAT TO DO WHILE ON A RETREAT

HOW YOU SPEND THE TIME ON YOUR RETREAT DEPENDS ON WHAT KIND OF PLACE AND RETREAT IT IS, BUT COMMON TO ALL VARIETIES IS THE CALL TO BE SERIOUSLY COMMITTED TO THE HOSPITALITY OFFERED. GUESTS FIT IN WITH THEIR HOST'S WAYS OF DOING THINGS AND DO NOT SEEK TO CHANGE THEM TO WAYS THEY THINK BETTER. MOREOVER, YOU ARE NOT JUST A GUEST BUT ALSO A PARTICIPANT. YOU ARE THERE, NOT TO BE WAITED ON, BUT TO BE TREATED EVEN MORE GENEROUSLY: AS ONE OF THE FAMILY FOR HOWEVER LONG YOUR STAY.

A retreat should be made in a spirit of curiosity. The experience is an unusual one; it challenges us to live differently and, in particular, more simply. The more you can hold onto a sense of adventure and interest, the more you will open yourself to the movement of the spirit.

Another way of thinking about the experience is to see the retreat as a kind of text you can read or listen to. During the times of silence, you can enter into your own inner conversation with the words addressed to you, either directly through the talks, worship, or guidance, or indirectly through a heightening of the senses on walks or meditation. If the retreat provides you with all sorts of "texts" to read, the most appropriate and creative response is for you to compose something in reply.

One of the most moving descriptions of a retreat I know (and accounts of other people's spiritual vacations do not always make the liveliest of reading!) is that of a few days in a Georgian monastery spent by the Russian priest Father Alexander Elchaninov when he was a schoolboy. What is striking about the report is that the young man seems to do nothing in particular during his stay except join in the life of the monks. He goes to services (which he finds boring), he does

some work—fetching water from a nearby stream, he goes for a walk, he thinks of home. But from his writing, you get an intense sense of place and experience. What made his short stay a true retreat was his willingness to accept the way things were, to "go with the flow," as we might say, in a place he had previously visited as a tourist but had felt drawn back to as a guest.

OBSERVING SILENCE

TRY TO BECOME AWARE OF THE MOMENTS OF SILENCE YOU EXPERIENCE DURING YOUR ORDINARY DAY. LIKELY TIMES ARE EARLY IN THE MORNING AND LATE AT NIGHT OR IN BREAKS WHEN COLLEAGUES LEAVE THE WORKPLACE. THERE ARE OFTEN QUIET MOMENTS DURING IN-BETWEEN TIMES, SUCH AS WHEN PEOPLE GOING TO WORK OR SCHOOL HAVE LEFT THE STREETS BUT SHOPPERS OR VISITORS HAVE YET TO APPEAR. IN YOUR MIND, RUN THROUGH THE COURSE OF A TYPICAL DAY AND IDENTIFY SUCH PERIODS. MAKE A MENTAL NOTE TO BE AWARE OF THEM THE FOLLOWING DAY.

Exercise

••• Get to know tranquil places near you, such as hidden gardens or peaceful buildings that are accessible to the public. Visit these occasionally to remind yourself of what silence is like.

••• Spend ten minutes or so in a quiet place trying to grasp just how silent it really is. What are the sounds that intrude? Are they still familiar ones, such as nearby heating or air-conditioning systems or moving traffic? Pay particular attention to occasional passing sounds, such as aircraft or flocks of birds. Later, return in your memory to the exercise and make a sound map of the place, using words or pictures to identify the various noises.

••• Find a place of almost total silence. This is more likely to be an insulated space in an office building than somewhere in open country. See how long you feel comfortable there. Make a note of the thoughts that intrude, particularly the disquieting ones. Resolve to work on coming to terms with their reasons for troubling you.

••• Create opportunities for what I like to call "warm" silences, quiet times in comfortable and familiar conditions. Mark the time as special by lighting a candle and dimming the lights; then allow yourself gently to recall similar peaceful moments in your history. Afterward, make a note of these peaceful times, too, in order to affirm them as just as real as the anxious times.

••• If you have a partner or close friend, agree to sit together quietly for a while, maybe in the warm conditions just described. Share your experiences simply without comment or criticism.

••• When conditions are not as comfortable, ask your partner or friend to help you be silent. Take turns reading to each other for ten minutes or so, perhaps during your meal the way members of a monastery traditionally do.

••• Agree to spend a certain part of the day in silence without talking unnecessarily and without listening to the radio or television. Again, share and note your experiences afterward.

READING INSPIRATIONAL TEXTS

WHEN YOU WITHDRAW, YOU DO NOT DO SO ALONE OR INTO EMPTINESS. AN IMPORTANT WAY OF RECALLING THIS TRUTH IS THROUGH MAKING USE OF INSPIRATIONAL TEXTS, WRITINGS THAT THE TRADITIONS RECOGNIZE AS SACRED OR THAT INDIVIDUALS EXPERIENCE AS SUCH.

You read such texts, not just for information or entertainment, but in order to meet the inspired voice behind them. Inspirational reading is a way of listening to the words rather than scanning them with the eyes, just as the retreat itself is a way of going deeper and developing awareness. Inspirational reading is quite simple:

Exercise

••• Identify a text to ponder and open it before you.

••• Still your body and mind as you seek to encounter the presence behind the text.

••• Read slowly through the text, pausing and restarting however seems right. Read as if you were listening to wise words of advice being offered to you personally by a respected teacher or guide.

••• Listen, not so much for ideas that engage the intellect, as for words or phrases that inspire or warm the spirit.

••• Hold on to those that touch you, and repeat them to yourself before moving on.

••• Do not worry about how much text you get through; rather, value with gratitude the way the words speak directly to you.

••• Later in the day, and especially before going to bed, briefly recall the words that struck you and still seem meaningful. Write them in your journal, perhaps adding a few words of personal response.

Because inspirational reading is not reading for information, it can provide an opportunity for exploring other traditions. However, it is probably closer to the spirit of the exercise to use texts from your own faith or ones you have come across naturally, rather than ones chosen deliberately to increase your knowledge.

You may wish to show reverence for texts that move you. In Christian churches, the Gospel book is often left open on a lectern with a light burning before it. Muslims place the Koran on a small folding wooden stand when reading it prayerfully. The Torah scroll in synagogues is kept in the sacred ark, and the text is not touched with the fingers but followed with a pointer, usually in the form of a human hand.

If you are using a variety of sources, you might not begin with a volume to revere but may want to create one of your own.

CONTEMPLATING DIVINE IMAGES

THE PRINCIPAL IMAGES OF THE SACRED TRADITIONS ARE IMMENSELY POWERFUL AND CARRY ALL SORTS OF MEANINGS, EVEN FOR NONBELIEVERS WHO, FOR HISTORICAL OR POLITICAL REASONS, MAY ASSOCIATE THE IMAGES WITH NEGATIVE CONNOTATIONS.

For devotees, images are sometimes so familiar they have all but lost their charge and potency. One purpose of a retreat is to provide spiritual exercises built around entering the power of the symbol, so that we may experience for ourselves something of what it represents.

In the Christian tradition, icons have been called windows into eternity, affording through their highly articulated form a kind of a glimpse of the divine. Often, these icons are abstract rather than representational of things in the real world. The icons of the Orthodox Christian tradition do not so much attempt to realistically depict their subject matter as to touch the believer in the way certain pieces of music are said to stir the soul.

In Tibetan Buddhism, practitioners visualize images of the virtues of the Buddha that they seek to make their own. They imagine themselves identifying with the image and so taking into themselves the qualities it represents.

Most of us will probably feel most comfortable with images that speak to us of the truths that the various traditions have in common.

The four basic elements figure in most traditions as symbolic of the divine ground of all there is and, more specifically in some, as aspects of the truth. Water, for instance, is used to represent the primeval turmoil of the universe and the healing and life-giving power of the divine in the world. Most traditions use it as a means for purification and restoration. Fire, on the other hand, is used to picture the energy of the divine acting in the world and upon individuals.

Having been brought up near the sea, I have always found water particularly inspiring. Over the years, I have gathered a small collection of images of lakes, streams, and rivers to help me enter into meditation and prayer. The flow of a river carries my thoughts in all sorts of directions, while the stillness of a pond offers constant reassurance.

In building up your own collection of images, choose those that are simple and unfussy and do not involve human figures likely to divert your thoughts. As always, make a note of how different scenes affect you. Occasionally, reflect on where these feelings and thoughts are coming from, whether they are a help or a hindrance to your spiritual development, and if you need to take some action to deal with them.

MEDITATION AND PRAYER

IN RECENT YEARS, MEDITATION HAS BEEN PROMOTED IN THE WEST AS A KIND OF RELAXATION EXERCISE FOR BUSY PEOPLE WHO FIND IT DIFFICULT TO REST. WE ARE RECOMMENDED TO INCORPORATE INTO OUR ROUTINE A LITTLE TIME EACH DAY— PERHAPS UP TO AN HOUR—TO SIT IN SILENCE AND FOCUS ON A WORD OR AN IMAGE. SCIENTIFIC EVIDENCE SUPPORTS THE VALUE OF MEDITATION AS A TOOL FOR PRODUCTIVITY AND EFFICIENCY AT WORK. NO DOUBT A RETREAT—A LONGER PERIOD OF MEDITATION—CAN BRING EVEN GREATER BENEFITS. BUT THIS IS NOT WHAT MEDITATION WAS ORIGINALLY ABOUT. INSTEAD, ITS PURPOSE WAS SPIRITUAL: TO WITHDRAW THE MIND FROM EVERYDAY CONCERNS SO THAT IT MIGHT COME INTO CONTACT WITH THE DIVINE.

There is nothing wrong with using meditation as a tool for healthier living in the world, so long as when we have achieved silence within ourselves we do not become deaf to the voice that calls to us there. This is the danger of trying to be at peace with ourselves: we may discover that we are being offered something altogether more exciting. In the silence, we meet God.

In religious traditions, meditation is part of prayer. Prayer is the way in which we get in touch with the divine. It has been called the "lifting of the heart to God" to emphasize that it is not just an intellectual activity but also one that involves our whole being. Prayer implies a belief and a relationship with God that makes communication with the divine conceivable and possible. It might involve asking God for protection and guidance, but at a deeper level prayer implies a calling to a stronger communion with the transcendent, just as a human loving relationship moves beyond conversation to a richer joy in each other's presence. Sometimes this deeper prayer is called "contemplation" or "mystical prayer," to distinguish it from common aspects of typical prayer such as praise, petition, and intercession.

But do not worry too much about terminology. Here, we will use *meditation* to mean various ways or methods of moving toward prayer or union with the divine.

Meditation originally meant to learn spiritual texts by heart by constantly repeating them, even to "enter into" them with your whole being—body as well as mind. One of the most fundamental techniques, though, is to concentrate on a single word or mantra. The best-known mantra is the sound "Om" or "Aum" from the Hindu tradition, but it is best to choose one from your own tradition or experience. The Catholic Benedictine monk John Main, who founded the Christian Meditation movement, recommended the Aramaic word *Maranatha*, which means, "Come, Lord!" If you do not identify deeply with a particular tradition, you could use something like "Holy" or "Spirit." Although you are not thinking about the meaning of the word, it is probably best to use one that suggests something outside of yourself rather than an aspect of life such as "love" or "peace."

Exercise

••• The technique of meditation is simple. Find the quietest place you can. Sit upright in a comfortable position on a cushion or chair—but not where you are likely to doze off! Take a deep breath and then breathe calmly and rhythmically. Close your eyes and begin to repeat your chosen word in your mind in tune with your breathing, concentrating on each syllable to the exclusion of all other thoughts. To begin with, try to maintain this practice for a set period of around twenty minutes.

••• At first, your task will be to concentrate on repeating the word; then it will be to fight off the distractions around you; and finally, it will be to keep going for the full period. The purpose, according to the Eastern Christian teaching, is to "bind the mind with one thought—the thought of the One."

••• As we become used to turning inward in silence, the next step is to extend the period of meditation by a few minutes or so until we are sitting for about fifty minutes. As this extra time exceeds the time of preparation, you begin to sense the stillness moving from the mind to the heart, so that it is becoming a quality of your whole being.

••• Meditation turns now into a waiting for the divine. It is a period of "attention," of mental alertness directed outward to the anticipated arrival of the loved one. It has been said that prayer—immediate contact with the divine—is something that "happens," that comes to us as a gift. The mind is less active now; the heart finds rest; the body may be moved to express the recognition and appreciation of the divine with a deep bow or prostration.

AIDS TO MEDITATION AND PRAYER

ON YOUR RETREAT, YOU MIGHT BE INTRODUCED TO MANY DIFFERENT MEDITATION PRACTICES. IT IS IMPORTANT TO FEEL COMFORTABLE WITH A CHOSEN METHOD OF PRAYER OR MEDITATION. AT THE BEGINNING, OR REALLY AT ANY POINT, YOU MIGHT WANT TO TRY OUT LESS FAMILIAR TECHNIQUES FROM TRADITIONS OTHER THAN YOUR OWN.

The Mantra

Certain sounds seem to strike to the depths of our being. It is almost as if they tune into our inner nature. The great traditions are all familiar with the idea of using a word or syllable as an aid to meditation or prayer. The best-known one is the sacred syllable "Om" employed in both Hinduism and Buddhism. It is considered to be the primordial sound of the universe. By concentrating on and linking it to the breath, the practitioner can achieve contact with the energy underlying creation. In Orthodox Judaism, the name of God may be neither spoken nor written; but, according to mystical teachers, it may be "sounded" internally during meditation. In Islam and Sikhism, God is said to have many names, and mystical teachers help seekers to identify an appropriate one for their own prayer.

Beads

Hindus and Buddhists move a string of beads through the fingers as a way of accompanying the repetition of the mantra, while those in Eastern Christianity use knotted ropes to count the saying of the Jesus Prayer ("Lord Jesus Christ, Son of God, have mercy on me, a sinner.").

In Tibetan, the word for telling the beads means to purr like a cat, suggesting that the meaning of the mantra is not so important. People who use beads find they become less conscious of the sounds they are reciting and more of the atmosphere created by them.

Touch Stones

Carry around a small stone as your personal link with the other dimensions of creation. A pebble or polished stone to move and sometimes squeeze in the hand can be both relaxing and conducive to concentration. A stone you have hallowed in this way could be placed as a symbol on a grave, for example, as people do in the Jewish tradition. In the ancient Celtic tradition, pilgrims would pile stones in cairns at sacred spots. In Tibet, prayer walls appear at the entrances to villages and temples and on bridges and hilltops. Often they are painted with a mantra to consecrate the natural landscape and inspire those passing by.

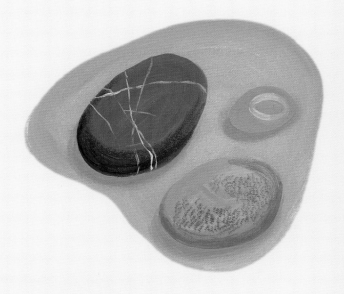

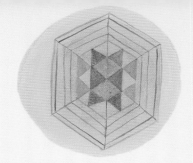

Shapes

The "yantra" is the less well-known visual equivalent of the mantra sound. The idea of substituting an image or symbol for an aspect of the divine is known to all traditions yet rarely discussed, largely because of the absence of a suitable word in English. For example, Christianity often returns to Greek and Latin for many of its concepts. The yantra is not any picture or literal representation, but more specifically an attempt to depict the spiritual reality geometrically or architecturally.

A Christian yantra, for instance, might be a triangle representing the mystery of the Trinity or a church laid out (as most are) in the shape of the cross—which is itself a yantra of Jesus' crucified body. The six-pointed Star of David has been interpreted in esoteric Judaism as representing the four corners of the world and the movement vertically to and from God the creator.

The psychologist C. G. Jung had a particular interest in the mandala, a design based on the circle but containing other shapes revolving around a central point. In Tibetan Buddhism, the mandala is everywhere in art. Monks painstakingly construct elaborate ones from grains of colored sand as exercises in patient contemplation. In meditation their purpose is to draw the mind away from diversities to the still center of the world. Jung believed that in Western terms mandalas could be said to have therapeutic value, and he encouraged his patients to draw and interpret them.

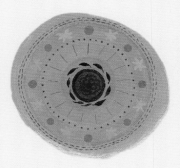

Smell and Taste

Guides to prayer and meditation rarely seem to say much about our sense of smell, yet fragrant-smelling flowers and plants are usually the first thing we think of when decorating a sacred space or marking a place out for prayer. Many traditions use incense to represent what the Bible calls the "odor of sanctity" or just to take away everyday aromas and remind the visitor that the space is set apart for a special purpose. They also use perfumed oils to anoint people who are consecrated to a special task, such as being a priest or soothing the sick.

Food plays a major part in world religions. Christians are invited in the Eucharist to "taste the Lord." Hindus offer all sorts of exotic delicacies before the images of the gods and then share them in worship.

As an exercise in spiritual gratitude and awareness, savor the smells and tastes of your food rather than just consuming it quickly. Think of those who do not have enough to eat. How can you help them?

A CHRISTIAN CONTEMPLATIVE RETREAT

IN 1521, INIGO LOPEZ, A NOBLEMAN FROM THE BASQUE COUNTRY OF NORTHERN SPAIN, WAS ABOUT THIRTY YEARS OLD WHEN HE WAS BADLY WOUNDED IN BATTLE, HIS RIGHT LEG SHATTERED BY A CANNONBALL. THE VICTORIOUS FRENCH ALLOWED HIM TO RETURN HOME TO LOYOLA, WHERE HE BEGAN A LONG AND PAINFUL CONVALESCENCE—HIS DAMAGED LEG HAVING TO BE BROKEN AGAIN TWICE IN ORDER TO BE SET PROPERLY.

Inigo, whose life until then had been dedicated to the so-called good things of life, had only some books about Christ and the saints to occupy his time. Over the months, he began to see that the saints he was reading about were also warriors and heroes. He was attracted to the idea of dedicating his life to the service of Christ, but he could not imagine giving up his old courtly ways.

On an excursion after his recovery, he had a religious argument with someone on the road. As the man rode off, Inigo felt his hand moving toward his dagger. Then he hesitated, torn between giving chase for the sake of honor and allowing the man the freedom to hold his own views. In the end, Inigo let his mule decide! When the mule chose to follow a path that led away from the antagonist, Inigo began to realize what his own calling was to be.

He exchanged his clothes with a beggar and then traveled on to Manresa, where he put up in an almshouse and later in a monastery. There he remained for a year in what became a retreat, spending long hours in prayer and experiencing strong feelings, both of his own inadequacy and of God's concern for him. Eventually, while resting by the river, the eyes of his understanding were opened, and it seemed as if he had become a new person. His profound, sudden sense of the closeness of God would inspire him for the rest of his life.

During his retreat, Inigo—or "Ignatius," as he would call himself—had recorded his experiences in a notebook that he later developed into a manual for helping others recognize and respond to the call of God in their lives.

The Spiritual Exercises of Saint Ignatius Loyola consists of a series of meditations and various "rules for the discernment of spirits;" that is, notes on how to interpret the spiritual movements experienced by someone making a retreat. Ignatius was very reluctant for his notes to be published in book form and always intended them primarily as suggestions for retreat-givers. Indeed, he recommends that retreats should be tailored to the needs of those making them, and, although the full exercises are described as thirty days spent apart from daily life, they might also be presented over a longer period for those who cannot take time out.

What has come to be called Ignatian Spirituality has been summarized as "finding God in all things." It uses every sort of spiritual exercise to help individuals rid themselves of attachment to vain pursuits and take up the challenge of finding the will of God for their own lives.

One of the central Ignatian exercises, for example, is the "Call of the King." It is given after retreat-takers have attempted to come to terms with their past lives without God and in opposition to God's intentions. Its purpose is not to force a change but to bring about a new awareness of the general, indeed cosmic, significance of our life choices.

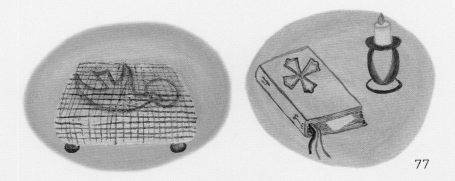

THE CALL OF THE KING

HERE ARE THE STEPS FOR PRACTICING THE CALL OF THE KING.

Exercise

••• Imagine that you are in the presence of a human king chosen by God, a king who enjoys the respect and homage of all good people.

••• Listen to the way this king speaks to his people and invites them to join him in some difficult but worthwhile task. Those who join him are warned they will face hardship, danger, and deprivation.

••• Now consider the derision and ridicule anyone who refused to follow such a devout king would receive.

••• Now repeat the exercise, replacing the earthly king with Christ and his mission to bring peace, love, and justice to the world.

••• Imagine Christ is calling you personally to assist him in this tremendous task.

••• Consider how no reasonable and well-intentioned person could possibly refuse such an invitation, despite the suffering that following Christ is bound to bring.

••• Think of how those who accept Christ's invitation not only labor with him but are also prepared to work against their own desires and ambitions.

The original form of this exercise is characteristic of the age of chivalry and clearly rooted in Inigo's own experience. Many today would have difficulty with the idea of obedience to a warrior-king. A modern adaptation might substitute a campaigner for the cause of the poor, or concentrate on the tasks rather than on the leader.

The distinctive Ignatian method, however, is as relevant now as it was when Inigo developed it. It involves entering deeply into the picture evoked through the imagination and applying each of the senses to the scene under consideration. The goal is to gain an impression, not only of what the scene would look like, but also of how it would sound, feel, and even smell to be there yourself.

A BUDDHIST MINDFULNESS RETREAT

IN HIS FIRST SERMON AFTER HIS ENLIGHTENMENT, THE BUDDHA EXPLAINED HIS TEACHING BY STATING FOUR FUNDAMENTAL TRUTHS: SUFFERING IS THE PRIMARY CHARACTERISTIC OF ALL BEINGS; SUFFERING IS THE RESULT OF DESIRE; SUFFERING WILL END WHEN DESIRE IS OVERCOME; AND THE WAY TO ACHIEVE THIS END IS BY FOLLOWING THE WAY OF THE BUDDHA. THIS PATH CAN BE SUMMARIZED AS HAVING A RIGHT UNDERSTANDING OF THE WAYS THINGS ARE AND A RIGHT WAY OF ACTING AS A CONSEQUENCE.

A Buddhist retreat is always a withdrawal from the desire that brings about suffering and a reaching toward the clarity of mind that the Buddha himself achieved and showed was possible for all people. Meditation is the principal route to this goal as well as the method by which we discover the truth of the teaching.

When I first came across the teaching of the Buddha, I found it hard to accept that suffering was the basic condition of existence. Things were not that bad, even at the worst of times. Was not life characterized by an absurd ambiguity in which pleasure and pain were mixed to a meaningless degree? How could desire be the cause of all the pain in the world? Was it not often a foundation for pleasure?

I made my first Buddhist retreat as a young student, under the guidance of a Tibetan lama who had come to live near my family's home. Some of my friends and I helped him and a group of exiles from the Chinese occupation of their country transform an old Scottish farmhouse into a meditation center. Located in an isolated valley, the house was reached by hitchhiking the few miles from the nearest railway station. I remember my first sight of the center with its tall prayer flags fluttering in the lowland breeze. Most of the other guests were also young people who were happy to sleep on mattresses on the floors of shared rooms.

We were given daily chores similar to the sort youth hostels used to assign as a condition of a traveler's stay. I worked for a while in the kitchen where vegetarian meals were prepared that surprised me with their variety and taste. We could spend time in the library or take walks in the nearby countryside, but the real purpose in being there was to participate in the four- or five-hour-long meditation sessions that took place from early in the morning until late in the evening.

I was a teenager, and it was a very new experience for me. I can still vividly recall entering the shrine room at around six in the morning for *puja*—the morning ceremony of dedication—wrapped in a blanket to keep off the cold. The formal procedure began with deep-voiced Tibetan chanting: "I take my refuge in the Buddha. I take my refuge in the *dharma*, or teaching. I take my refuge in the *sangha*, the community of all those following the way." Then we sat for an hour or so concentrating on breathing slowly and steadily, trying to overcome the pain of sitting cross-legged or in some approximation of the lotus position.

Occasionally the lama would address us at the beginning of a meditation period. When a new group arrived, he would warn us against drink and drugs. The business of meditation was a serious one and not just the latest fashion for middle-class youth. In his country, the opportunity for spiritual retreat was highly prized and becoming increasingly restricted.

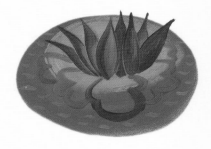

The teaching I remember most clearly was that the Buddha nature is possible for us all to attain and that the many—to my mind—strange images decorating the shrine room were best viewed as aspects of our own thoughts. These images represented various ways of thinking that might inspire or impede us on our journey to mindfulness—the total awareness that is the goal of the Buddhist practitioner, consisting of both detachment from desire and clarity of vision. Mindfulness involves awareness of the body and of the mental processes of feeling and thinking. Meditation is a concentrated effort to bring about mindfulness in daily life.

As a preparatory exercise, or at the start of a meditation period, try to become exceptionally aware of your body. Move in your thoughts from your head to your chest and stomach, then from limb to limb to the tips of your fingers and toes. Next, try to get in touch first with your feelings and then with your thoughts, but without lingering on any single one. Just try to accept that you are here now and that this is how it is for you. Then move into an exercise that helps you exclude all of these thoughts and sensations, such as one we looked at in the section, Aids to Meditation and Prayer. At the end of your sitting, return through the thoughts, feelings, and bodily sensations into your ordinary waking consciousness. Find odd moments in the day to gently repeat a simple form of this exercise, to increase your awareness of the gift of life and the beauty of the world.

A NATURE RETREAT

I USED TO BE TROUBLED BY STORIES IN THE SACRED SCRIPTURES THAT REPRESENTED HOLY MEN AND WOMEN OVERCOMING THE FORCES OF NATURE OR BEING ABLE TO CONVERSE WITH ANIMALS AND BIRDS. I FOUND THEM DIFFICULT TO USE IN PRAYER AND MEDITATION, BECAUSE I IMAGINED THEY WERE BEING HELD UP AS GOALS FOR THE SPIRITUAL SEEKER. SHOULD I BE SEEKING SUCH POWERS FOR MYSELF? HOW WOULD THE ABILITY TO WALK ON WATER OR KEEP WARM IN THE SNOWS DRESSED ONLY IN A COTTON SHEET BENEFIT HUMANKIND? WHAT WOULD I HAVE TO SAY TO THE CREATURES ON THE SEASHORE? WHAT KIND OF A GOD WAS IT WHO WANTED US TO HANDLE SNAKES?

Later I came to understand that these stories were pictures of how humans should relate to the natural world. The holy person is not so much an extraordinary person as an image of what we are all meant to be. When the saints perform their marvelous deeds, they reveal not their power over nature but their harmony with it. Theirs seem like magical powers because we are caught up in a world of rivalry and conflict; but for those who lack envy and are at peace, the deeds of saints are images of the cooperative and relational character of reality.

Perhaps true harmony will not be restored in the universe until it reaches its consummation; but by tasting it in the midst of our ordinary existence, we can contribute to its appearance. By coming into a harmonious relationship with nature, we can get a sense of how life is meant to be.

Today there are many establishments that offer the "back to nature" experience. Looking through their information and statements on the Internet, I can only be impressed by their facilities and locations. At the same time, part of me feels that really getting back to nature involves subjecting yourself to the elements. I am not suggesting that you put yourself in danger, but it does seem important to get in touch with nature's power as well as with its beauty.

My favorite places for experiencing the elements have been in the mountains and by the sea. I am fortunate to have had the use of simple houses that don't offer a lot of luxuries and yet are comfortable enough and adequately equipped. In one case, the house was still in the process of construction, and visitors earned their keep through whatever labor they could offer. In another, water had to be drawn from a pump in the yard, and cooking done on a wood-burning stove. My favorite was one where I had to respond to the weather by opening or closing shutters and roof panels. Through such small chores, I was reminded that nature is not at our disposal; it does not owe us anything, and we should only take from it what we need.

In selecting a setting for your retreat, try, according to your own needs and abilities, to find somewhere that you can maintain or improve in some small way. Look for a place where some of your needs have to be satisfied by daily tasks, such as collecting wood, or where you can improve the quality of your stay by ordering and collecting fresh milk or bread.

Exercise

••• Think of the different ways you can experience the elements. If you are near the sea, observe the movement of the tides. Take a walk along the shoreline in the morning and evening and notice how the size of the coast changes through the day. Take your shoes off and walk into the water to feel how its temperature changes. See if you can rent a small boat to feel the undulations of the water, and imagine yourself farther out at its mercy. Look for sea life in the rocks and pools and human life in ships on the horizon. Listen to the sound of the waves and see how far they carry back into land. The sea can never fail to invoke feelings of awe and wonder.

••• In their way, the mountains, too, emphasize our finitude. Their heights may be beyond our reach. Some of the routes through or over them will be impassable. They remind us of the beginnings of the world when the rocks and earth were being formed.

••• If you are in the mountains, identify a safe walk and take yourself to where you become a speck in the distance to the nearest dwelling. Remember to keep an eye on the weather conditions and wear the right clothing. Watch for the creatures that make their home there, particularly the large birds of prey that delight in the wind currents created by the hills and have no fear of the heights and isolation.

••• Seek out an "oasis" in the locality where water, vegetable, and animal life seem to come harmoniously together. Is this a place that humans have respected or desecrated? How can you sanctify it for yourself?

••• A particular kind of nature retreat is inspired by the native North American idea of the "Vision Quest," but is known also in first nation Australian and other traditions. Under the guidance of an experienced leader, either individually or in a group, the retreatant spends some time getting used to the local circumstances and climate and to a simplified and basic diet. This is followed by time spent alone in very basic accommodation or even in the open air. The idea is that the most basic form of material living will help to bring out the retreatant's obscured spiritual nature often in a very striking and perceptible way. These "visions" that result are shared with the leader and group who try to help the individual understand their significance for everyday life. The getting back-to-nature experience can be amplified or supplemented in many different ways. The "walkabout" might be made on horseback with the animal's needs having to be met as well. The time might be spent in a boat on water or in a cave in a mountainous environment. It is very important that proper safety precautions are taken and everything is undertaken under expert guidance.

DEALING WITH DIFFICULTIES

IF YOU ARE FACING DIFFICULTIES ON RETREAT, YOU OUGHT TO CONGRATULATE YOURSELF! IT IS A GREAT ACHIEVEMENT TO HAVE ACTUALLY MADE IT THIS FAR. SO MANY PEOPLE LONG FOR TIME APART WITHOUT EVER ACHIEVING IT. HERE YOU ARE, WORRYING ABOUT HOW HARD IT IS!

Furthermore, difficulties are one of the gifts of the retreat. They are ways of identifying what parts of yourself and your life you need to work on.

When your car breaks down, for instance, you look for what is wrong and try to fix it. Actually, it is not the entire car that is out of order but some part of it, and, as we know from experience, that part is usually a pretty small one. A breakdown reveals just how important even the tiniest part of a machine is. It is the same with us. If we cannot pray or meditate or concentrate on some important text or idea, it is not because we are failures or spiritual rejects. It may just be that some small part of us needs to be thought about or changed.

Everyone knows that the hardest part of an activity is in making a start and that, even when that initial hurdle is overcome, the problems seem to come quickly and in every shape. It is as if all the difficulties we might face want to reveal themselves to us as soon as they can. The ancient spiritual writers say that the demons clamor to show their faces to the spiritual beginner because they are fighting among themselves to be the one who discourages her. Because they are all making a din at once, they sound noisier and seem more dangerous than they really are.

Again, it is like the way a new car frustratingly always seems to have something wrong with it within weeks of delivery and has to go back to the garage. But after all the problems are worked out, you can usually hope for a smooth ride for some time to come. Similarly, if you can face up to your demons at the start of your retreat, they will understand that you mean business.

The demons reveal their character in the way they squabble among themselves. They also reveal that the principal factor that interferes with our spiritual concentration is our relations with other people. Whatever form distraction takes, it very frequently has its root in some disordered relationship. If there is one single preparation you should make before going on retreat, it is to do your best to straighten out any differences you have with others.

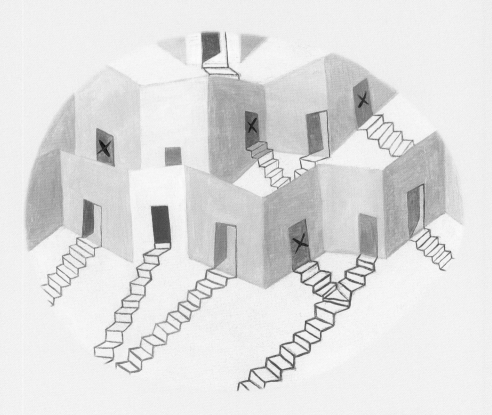

GETTING TO KNOW YOURSELF

THE TRADITIONAL LITERATURE ON SPIRITUALITY DEVOTES MUCH DISCUSSION TO WHAT IS CALLED THE "MOVEMENT OF THE SPIRITS." SUCH TERMINOLOGY REMINDS US THAT WHEN WE PRAY OR MEDITATE, WE ARE OPENING UP, BOTH TO WHAT IS DEEP WITHIN OUR OWN BEINGS AND TO A REALITY OUTSIDE OURSELVES.

When we feel calm and comforted, we could say it is because the "good spirit" is working within us, and when we are disturbed or aggravated, it is because the "bad" spirit is placing obstacles in our way. However, it is important not to assume that this straightforward

reading is necessarily the correct one. The bad spirit is by definition a spirit of deception and therefore seeks to disguise its activity by confusing and misleading us. It may sometimes bring a sense of consolation in order to make us feel complacent and oblivious to any need to make changes in our lives. Similarly, the good spirit is truthful and will reveal our shortcomings to us.

The movement of the spirits is the very stuff of spirituality. The deepest purpose of the retreat is to bring that movement to our attention so that we can understand ourselves and make progress. This is the material that we identify in reviewing our times of prayer and meditation and that we bring to spiritual direction.

We sometimes say "the spirit moved me" to do such and such, by which we mean we are not quite sure why we did it but somehow felt we had to. The expression has a slightly comic ring to it, as if we are finding an excuse for doing something that appears out of character. What we should be doing is trying to identify which spirit has moved us. The way to do that is through deep reflection on the direction in which we feel pulled. It can often happen to retreat-takers, for example, that they feel called upon to change their lives in some dramatic way. If you have such a sense, you need seriously to question whether such a change is in keeping with other movements in your awareness and how it would affect other people. It is very important not to allow the "moving spirit" to be an excuse for acting irrationally. We deceive ourselves if we think that something is right just because it feels right. The spirit is not opposed to reason, and we must make every effort to justify our actions by the proper moral and public standards.

REVIEWING YOUR ACCOMPLISHMENTS

AT THE END OF THE RETREAT, IT IS VERY IMPORTANT TO MAKE SOME TIME TO REVIEW HOW IT WENT. I CANNOT STRESS ENOUGH HOW IMPORTANT THIS ACTIVITY IS. YOU HAVE MADE TIME IN YOUR BUSY LIFE FOR SOMETHING YOU BELIEVE TO BE IMPORTANT; NOW IS THE MOMENT TO REFLECT ON HOW YOU HAVE BEEN CHANGED. THIS REVIEW IS LIKE SAVORING THE TASTE AT THE END OF A MEAL, GIVING THANKS TO THE COOK, DISCUSSING THE INGREDIENTS AND METHODS OF PREPARATION, AND TAKING AWAY THE RECIPE FOR FUTURE USE. WITHOUT SUCH CONSIDERATION, THE MEAL IS DEVALUED, REDUCED TO A MERE REFUELING.

Exercise

••• Set aside a serious period for the review. Its length will best be determined by the length of your retreat: say, a half hour for a day, and an hour or more for several days. But be flexible; if you find yourself needing more time, resolve to take it later. Do not tire yourself straining to recall what happened several days ago. The review is a time to allow memories to emerge gently and naturally.

••• Begin by reminding yourself of how you came to go on retreat in the first place. How did you hear about the possibility? What was it that clicked with you and made you want to take a retreat?

••• Did you have a particular purpose or issue in mind when you embarked on the retreat? Do not ask immediately whether you achieved resolution; just remind yourself of your purpose.

••• Looking back, what feeling would you say generally sums up the spirit of the retreat for you? Was it a positive experience?

••• What images or ideas have been evoked? What connection is there between these images and your daily life?

••• Has the retreat inspired you to live differently in some way?

••• Compare the direction you feel the retreat has inspired you to move in with your original purpose for making it.

••• Do you feel you are being called to repeat this exercise or explore different ones?

••• Give thanks for the opportunity to make the retreat and for all who made it possible.

••• Write a paragraph summing up your review, and return to it occasionally to consider its continuing influence in your life.

PART 4

retreats
for every
purpose

TIME OUT FOR SPIRITUAL GROWTH

THINK ABOUT THE VACATIONS YOU HAVE TAKEN. WHEN I WAS GROWING UP OUR FAMILY HOLIDAYS ALTERNATED BETWEEN THE CAMPING ROAD TRIP AND THE COUNTRY COTTAGE. WHEN WE RENTED A COTTAGE, IT WAS USUALLY NOT PARTICULARLY FAR FROM HOME—JUST ENOUGH TO TAKE US BEYOND THE SIGHTS OF OUR DAY-TO-DAY EXPERIENCE AND INTRODUCE US TO OTHERS. WE WOULD MAKE EXCURSIONS TO PLACES NEARBY AND SPEND THE WHOLE DAY VISITING PLACES OF LOCAL INTEREST SUCH AS MUSEUMS OR GALLERIES.

As I look back now, I realize with some surprise that I have chosen to almost replicate my childhood vacations in my adult life. As a student, I made a series of intensive journeys by train across Europe; afterward, I found ways of making extended stays for work or study in places beyond the usual holiday routes. The only principal difference between my adult and childhood experiences was that in later years I always traveled alone. I do not think of myself as a particularly widely traveled person, but I like to believe that I have some understanding of other cultures and ways of life.

Although I have a certain experience of retreat-taking and giving, it was only when I came to write this section that I began to see strongly the personal connection between vacations and vacations for the spirit. Looking over and writing about my experiences became an exercise that I would suggest you do, too. It helped me see more clearly how ordinary the desire is to take a retreat—which is, after all, a vacation. But I also saw the imprint of my childhood experiences on my later explorations. Whenever I have taken time out for spiritual growth or for dealing with a particular event or experience, my reflections and thoughts have derived from and invoked memories of earlier vacations. In a sense, any time out has been a continuation of every other time out, and together they make an alternative history of my life. Whenever I go on a retreat, I am returning to that other side of myself that has stepped out of daily life—on the one hand, to escape from it and be somewhere else; on the other, to restructure my place within it.

I learned, also, that there can be various kinds of retreat for different times of our lives and different people. A retreat need not take the form of remaining concentrated in one place. It can be more like my camping vacations: moving from place to place, concentrating on heightening your awareness of the journey, and measuring, as it were, your moods and feelings. The two types of vacation are images of the two essential aspects of the retreat: the experience itself and a deep attentiveness toward how it moves you.

Now reflect on the time-outs in your own life. Did your childhood create a pattern that you took up and repeated or a routine that you reacted against? Does your response suggest to you appropriate ways of taking a spiritual vacation? Should you seek an individual or communal experience, a purely meditative one, or one that involves some sort of activity? Is what you want available, or might you have to devise something for yourself?

RETREATS AT TIMES OF LOSS OR CHANGE

THE LOSS OF A LOVED ONE TURNS US INWARDS. WE ARE NUMBED BY THEIR DEPARTURE, AND THE FORMALITIES OF THE FUNERAL SEEM TO BE OVER VERY QUICKLY. OUR CULTURE HAS ALMOST FORGOTTEN HOW TO MOURN. YOU ARE EXPECTED TO PUT YOUR GRIEF BEHIND YOU AND GET ON WITH LIFE AS SOON AS POSSIBLE. BUT OFTEN, THE SHOCK AND CONSEQUENCES OF A DEATH CAN HAVE THEIR GREATEST IMPACT WHEN THE PUBLIC PROCEEDINGS ARE OVER, AND THEY CAN CONTINUE FOR A LONG TIME AND AFFECT INDIVIDUALS IN DIFFERENT WAYS.

When someone of your acquaintance dies—even if you have not been close to them—the relationship is immediately frozen. It does not change from what it had been on that last day, and you are left to cope with the feelings that remain. For most of us, the overwhelming emotion is that of regret. If only we had sorted out those little differences and misunderstandings. Now it is too late.

Even if you have participated in all the memorial events after a death, it is still appropriate to spend a short time on your own reflecting on your loss. Set aside initially just a few minutes to sit in a quiet place. Place in front of you something that links you with the lost one: a photograph, if possible, or a souvenir of some shared experience. Gently allow your memories to surface and present themselves. Try to recall your friend's voice and manner. Recall how you met and got to know each other, some of the times you spent together, and the last occasion when you had real contact.

It is important to recognize, too, that you might have strong feelings of loss after the departure of even someone you had not seen for a long time or who had largely ceased to be a part of your life. Sometimes you discover that someone you hardly knew had touched you in a profound way.

As you dedicate this time to their memory, try to identify how you feel about the person. Is a brief period enough, or do you want to spend a longer time recalling them? Have you identified a particular moment or issues that are blocking your return to the world without them? There may be practical steps you can take to make up for past wounds caused or received. If not, some kind of symbolic act of forgiveness or apology may suffice.

Perhaps a short period of reflective mourning seems sufficient at the time, but later you begin to feel haunted by the memory of the deceased.

For instance, I remember that, after the death of someone I had known deeply but not seen for years, I would constantly find myself thinking about how my actions and decisions would have affected them. If I bought something, I would find myself thinking about showing it to them and seeking their opinion. For a moment, their

presence in my life seemed real to me again. I could begin to imagine I was actually able to see them or speak to them.

Here's another example: After the death of my mother a few years ago, I had the experience of thinking I had seen her again. Usually she would be in a crowd on the street, and I would be a short distance away, in a car or looking out a window from the floor above. I would set out to meet her, taking a step or two before realizing it could not be her. That was all. I never otherwise imagined she was still alive or ever found myself taking her reactions into account when I made decisions.

In reflecting on these two personal "hauntings," I came to see that the important thing was the feelings evoked, rather than the mysterious quality of the experiences. Particularly in the case of my deceased friend, it was as if my interior was making up for our lack of contact in later years but in a way entirely in accordance with the earlier ones. I felt I was being shown that the later distance between us did not matter; the relationship remained the same.

I have spoken about the loss of family and friends, but sometimes less obvious causes can also cause us grief and despair. Every loss, the psychologists tell us, invokes deep memories of our infantile separation from our mothers. They should, then, all be taken seriously. Once again, if something affects you negatively, I strongly recommend that you work on it.

Because time spent in a retreat is a time of reflection, hidden or half-forgotten feelings might emerge in our prayers or meditation. At many centers, trained and experienced guides are available to help people through whatever is being invoked. If not, make use of your notebook to brainstorm and free-associate thoughts and feelings to help identify the true nature of the manifestation. Always remember that perhaps you are being called to celebrate as much as to mourn, to rejoice as much as to feel regret. The task is to find the best way to move on.

THE WALKING RETREAT

IN OLD TIBET, IT IS SAID THAT THERE WERE ADEPTS WHO COULD WALK OR RUN FOR DAYS AT A TIME WITHOUT STOPPING FOR FOOD AND WATER. WITH PRACTICE AND TRAINING, THEY COULD MAINTAIN A FAST AND STEADY PACE AND SEEMED TO BOUNCE ACROSS THE LANDSCAPE LIKE RUBBER BALLS. THIS IS NOT WHAT IS MEANT BY A WALKING RETREAT.

A vacation for the spirit combines well with the kind of country or mountain walking many of us enjoy and look to for exercise and pleasure. As with any other kind of retreat, plan a walking tour in advance: arrange for accommodations, consider provisions, and decide on a route, which may involve visiting certain places of interest or following a particular trail. One of the most important parts of the preparation is the schedule—working out how far can be covered each day and whether there are alternatives if the weather deteriorates or conditions prove difficult.

I turned a walk in a local area of beauty into a retreat by spotting on a large-scale map a remarkable number of ancient standing stones and circles. In their isolation and bleak grandeur, these are places of power whatever your belief system. Coming from the time before recorded history, they are by definition places of mystery, and few could fail to feel a sense of awe standing alone in such a place. As I traveled between them and spent more days on my own, I felt drawn into the mystery of my own being. The heavier my body became as I tramped from stone to stone, the lighter my spirit seemed.

There is a type of city walker known by the untranslatable French word *flaneur*. It means something like a wandering observer or street "detective." The flaneur allows himself to drift through the city streets until his attention is caught by some object, scene, or display. He then examines it thoroughly, trying to read from it the secrets of the place and time.

A walking retreat in town could take the form of a pilgrimage to a church or temple, or to a powerful natural feature such as a hill or river. In an old city, such places probably had spiritual significance in the distant past. As you walk, open yourself to the discovery of previously overlooked features of the streetscape, and ponder why this shop name or that vista has revealed itself to you.

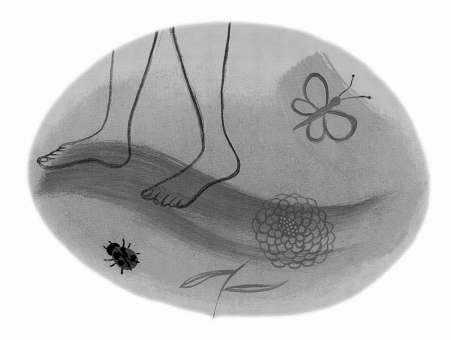

THE GROUP RETREAT

EVERY YEAR THE SCHOOL I AM CLOSELY INVOLVED WITH HAS WHAT IT CALLS A "VISION DAY." INSTEAD OF MEETING FOR SEVERAL HOURS IN THE SCHOOL LIBRARY ON AN EVENING WHEN, FRANKLY, EVERYONE IS TIRED, WE MEET ON THE WEEKEND. WE ARE FORTUNATE IN THAT SEVERAL TIMES ONE OF THE PARENTS WHO OWNS A HOTEL HAS MADE HIS FACILITIES AVAILABLE TO US, SO WE HAVE NOT NEEDED TO WORRY ABOUT REFRESHMENTS AND TIDYING UP. ALSO, THE BUILDING IS IN ANOTHER PART OF TOWN, WHICH IMMEDIATELY HELPS US GET A PERSPECTIVE ON SOME OF THE IMPORTANT ISSUES WE NEED TO DISCUSS. THAT IT IS NEAR WHERE SOME OF THE STUDENTS LIVE OFFERS YET OTHER BENEFITS.

The group retreat is an idea you may want to suggest for your own work group or volunteer organization. Or maybe you belong to a social group that would be intrigued by the idea of spending some reflective time away together.

Sometimes centers offer retreats or quiet days for particular types of people: men, women, students, charity workers, and so on; but what I have in mind here is people who identify with each other but may actually have very different roles. The average office or workplace, for instance, is comprised of a group of people of different ages and from different backgrounds engaged in various tasks for varying pay. A group who went to school together will have a strong bond uniting them but differ in almost every other way.

A vision-day retreat can take people out of their normal circumstances, often to help them meet in a significant way for the first time, regardless of how long they may have been acquainted.

A small planning group could compose a timetable that would allow individuals to spend short periods together—fifty minutes works well—and then take a short break before rearranging. Maintain a rule of silence during the day except in the sharing sessions and in a final social meeting over refreshments. You might want to ban all conversation about work so that colleagues discover each other's passions and interests.

One way to facilitate such sharing is to begin each session by asking people to talk about themselves to a partner who then introduces them to the group. The first person then has an opportunity to make corrections, and the others to ask questions before moving on.

A final session could ask each member to offer their vision for the group's future (rather than their criticisms of its past and present). To make it easier, this envisioning could be done in writing and the ideas put on display at the social gathering.

THE FAMILY RETREAT

WHEN WE TALK ABOUT WESTERN FAMILY, TODAY WE ARE USUALLY REFERRING TO THE SO-CALLED "NUCLEAR" FAMILY, OF PARENTS AND CHILDREN. IN THIS MODERN FAMILY EVERYONE ELSE IN THE WIDER CIRCLE IS KNOWN AS A "RELATIVE." IN FORMER TIMES, "CLAN GATHERINGS" WOULD HAVE BEEN COMMON. EVERYONE IN THE WIDEST FAMILY CIRCLE WOULD HAVE TURNED OUT FOR "FAMILY" EVENTS SUCH AS WEDDINGS. TODAY, COUPLES MAY CELEBRATE THEIR MARRIAGE WITH THEIR FRIENDS AND SOMETIMES ONLY THE CLOSEST RELATIVES ARE INVITED.

There are a number of ways of rediscovering what we used to mean by the word family. Try some ideas to draw the family together or bring them together in a form of "retreat."

Exercise

••• Draw a family tree. This is something that individuals tend to do as a hobby later in life when almost everyone named on the tree is gone or out of contact. There is something rather sad about finding out who you are by finding out who your relatives, past or present, are. Building on the idea of the family tree is to actually bring the people in your family together. Even in today's fragmented world, some of your relatives may possibly live in a cluster or two in a few localities.

••• Make a start just by calling them to find out who is still in touch with whom. Plot this information on your tree. Follow up with visits to likely aunts or uncles who sound enthused about your project. When you get into genealogy, you usually find that someone has been there before you!

••• Invite relatives who have never met or not seen each other for a long time to an informal social gathering on neutral ground. There can often be "issues" in families, so people need to be able to move around and change places or make excuses if they need to leave. A grand reunion banquet might not be the best place to start!

••• Work up gradually to the idea of a night or two away together. I arranged for some of my relatives to do so in a small guest house in the place we knew one side of the family had lived a century ago but no one resided now. We had an immediate common interest in visiting places in old photographs, features of the area that must have been known to great-great-grandparents, and, of course, the graveyard. After such excursions with your own family, allow time for a sharing session each evening. Suggest that someone write up the event or gather contributions, however small, from each participant.

THE PARTNERSHIP RETREAT

AN ANNIVERSARY OF MEETING, MARRYING, OR MAKING A SERIOUS COMMITMENT TO YOUR PARTNER IS A GOOD TIME TO REFRESH AND REINVIGORATE A RELATIONSHIP.

Exercise

••• The first step is to agree with your partner on a date for the retreat. Make sure to do so far in advance, so that both of you can be certain to be free and will have ample opportunity to make the necessary arrangements.

••• Next, prepare for the day with a couple of get-togethers over a meal. Inasmuch as you are entering into a creative process together, it would be good to mirror your intention by sharing the preparations and ingredients for the meal or by taking turns doing so.

••• Treat these get-togethers as anticipations of the actual retreat day. Plan a fixed time out of your routine to spend together, including the meal. If you live together, for example, set aside two hours to eat, clean up, and sit together. Agree in advance to share all the work.

••• When you are ready, sit opposite each other, extend your hands so that they touch without gripping, close your eyes, and remain for a minute or two in silence. You might feel self-conscious at first, but do not make too much of it. Think of it as how you might sit when waiting for some news or anticipating some result: As soon as word comes, you forget all about the tension of waiting!

••• The first time you and your partner meet this way, gently take turns saying in a few words about what you hope to gain from the retreat. Set aside about half the time for this exchange. It is

important to receive all ideas without comment or criticism. Ask only for clarification—particularly if what your partner has to say sounds hurtful to you. Then use the rest of the time for practical questions. There is a lot to be said for going away from home to somewhere like a hotel where your ordinary needs will be met and you can concentrate on your relationship. Retreat centers do not usually work well for couples!

••• During the next planning session, make a schedule for the retreat time. Set aside periods for walking and sitting together. You may want to construct a framework for reviewing your life together. As you practiced before, take turns in speaking rather than engaging in dialogue. Remind your partner of the positive moments you have shared. Spend short periods of silence in both the morning and the evening to repeat your partner's words to yourself. Then at the end of the day, repeat the words that have most moved you to your partner with gratitude.

••• Finish at the time you agreed on by giving each other a small gift.

THE CITY
RETREAT

IN THE PAST, THE CITY WAS THOUGHT OF AS A PLACE OF
SAFETY AND REFUGE FROM THE PERILS OF THE COUNTRYSIDE—
THE DOMAIN OF WILD BEASTS AND OUTLAWS. THE WORD
CIVILIZED ORIGINALLY MEANT "OF THE CITY" AND
"URBANE," IN THE SENSE OF HAVING POLITE
AND COURTEOUS MANNERS. FOR MANY
PEOPLE TODAY, THE CITY HAS A RATHER
NEGATIVE IMAGE. OUR THOUGHTS GO
QUICKLY TO THE PROBLEMS OF THE
INNER CITY, URBAN DECAY, AND THE
DANGERS OF DESERTED STREETS.
THIS IS A VERY MODERN IMAGE.

Cities began as markets, places where
country folk brought their produce to
be sold and where manufactured
goods and luxuries could be
obtained. They were also places of
entertainment and education. The
city was *many* places, whereas the
village, often dependent on a single
product, was only one. Civilization
was the consequence of different
kinds of people coming together,
living and working alongside each
other, and learning each other's
language and customs.

Although the city might at first seem
an unlikely place to make a retreat, in reality
it offers particular opportunities and resources for

spiritual withdrawal. The size and variety of cities provide all sorts of stimuli for our imagination. Its anonymity and tolerance allow us to be ourselves without attracting curiosity or comment.

Most of us live in or near the city, yet few of us truly know it well. We tend to be familiar with our own districts, the places where we live or work, the routes we take between the two. If to "withdraw" is to become "aware," we would do well to gain a sense of our city.

The city has sometimes been compared to the human body. If we want to get an idea of how well we are, of our strengths and limitations, we have to look at our bodies as a whole. But through our bodies we inhabit a world, and so we must also take into account the state of that world to complete the picture of our own health.

Exercise

••• The obvious way to get a sense of the city is by looking at a map, seeing how the city divides up into different districts and how they are linked to one another. Explore how the various areas got their names and what led to their development. Remember, this is not a local history project but an exercise in awareness. Think of the city as a living organism—its river and tributaries as its veins and blood vessels, the built-up areas and open spaces as its limbs and lungs. Ask yourself where the heart of your city is. Is it the financial center, the shopping district, or something more symbolic, such as a cathedral or palace?

••• What is the spiritual identity of your city, and how has it changed over the years? How many different traditions are represented? Where are they located? Where are their holy places? Are there remains of, or monuments to, now-vanished communities? What became of them? Mark on your map your new picture of the spiritual geography of your city.

••• Now consider your personal city. Transfer the picture of that to your map and see how it coincides with its sacred topography. Visit the holy sites on your doorstep as an exercise in recognizing what has been called "heaven-in-the-ordinary."

It may be that in doing this exercise you will discover places that speak to you and seem to beg you to rest for a while and hear their stories. But for the most part, this is an exercise in tuning the spiritual senses, a kind of warming up for your personal city retreat. The point is to try to see the city in a new light and yourself in a new relationship with it. And the best way of doing that is to wander the city, exploring its nooks and back streets, seeing what lies behind its main roads and facades.

If you live in an old and unplanned city, you will almost certainly come across half-forgotten spaces—churchyards or bits of garden, perhaps, known to local office workers who eat their lunch there, but empty for most of the time. Such places provide ideal locations for you to spend a short time on your own. Places where people come and go and that are are lived in, often seem more inviting for meditation than ones that have been abandoned.

The rhythm of the city provides an opportunity for building up a discipline of regular withdrawal. Create your own routine of spending a few moments a day or week in a treasured place. That way you can sanctify it for yourself and for your future use when you might need a place of retreat for celebration or remembrance. Use one of the awareness exercises above to consecrate your chosen space.

Lastly, remember the positive nature of the city I mentioned above. Much of what goes on may seem dedicated to acquisition and material values, but bless your city for the good it also does and for the well-being of those who work there.

THE ARTISTIC RETREAT

THE NINETEENTH-CENTURY CRITIC JOHN RUSKIN DISTINGUISHES BETWEEN THOSE WHO LOOK AND THOSE WHO SEE. HIS POINT IS THAT YOU CAN LOOK AT SOMETHING WITHOUT ACTUALLY SEEING IT, HAVE IT BEFORE YOUR EYES WITHOUT NOTICING IT. HE EVEN SUGGESTS THAT THOSE WHO SET OUT TO INVESTIGATE A PARTICULAR SIGHT OFTEN FAIL TO SEE IT. SEEING, HE SAYS, IS REALLY A CREATIVE ACTIVITY: THE BEST WAY OF SEEING AN OBJECT IS TO DRAW IT; A SURE WAY OF MISSING IT IS TO TAKE A PHOTOGRAPH.

A retreat is a creative vacation. It is a time for making an effort that is different from the way you normally expend your energy. Artistic activity—painting, sculpting and so on—is also a way of "going beyond" yourself, with clear links to the nature of a retreat.

Many schools and colleges offer, for example, painting vacations during breaks in which your domestic needs are met and time and guidance is provided for your work. And some retreat centers combine such vacations with spiritual exploration.

For those of us who are visual rather than literary thinkers, sketches and doodles can be the ways we record and respond to our moods and feelings in prayer and meditation. Like journaling with words, compiling a sketchbook can be a way of opening up to our depths and exploring our relationships. Even if you do not consider yourself talented, a sketchbook can be a place for collecting images torn from magazines and catalogs to create an atmosphere or act as a source of inspiration. Designers of clothes and furniture compile such albums to inspire their own work. They do not copy what they include, but by juxtaposing colors, patterns, and shapes that appeal to them, they consolidate and refine their own taste and move beyond such images to give birth to their own creations.

The wonderful illustrations in this book may give you some idea of how your own pictures might express your inner life, and you could use them as a starting point for your deliberations. Always remember, though, that a creative response is the most appropriate and authentic one to a piece of art. Look and see; then make your own.

THE MUSICAL RETREAT

SILENCE LIES AT THE HEART OF THE RETREAT, SO IT MIGHT SEEM THAT MUSIC COULD HAVE NO PART IN ONE. HOWEVER, THERE ARE TIMES BEFORE, DURING, AND AFTER A RETREAT WHEN MUSIC MIGHT INDEED HAVE A ROLE. ESSENTIALLY, THESE TIMES SERVE THE PURPOSE OF FRAMING THE SILENCE SO THAT IT CAN BE ENTERED INTO AND ENJOYED MORE EFFECTIVELY.

Sometimes I have arrived at a retreat center for a group experience to find music being played in the reception room as the group gathered. For those who had not made a retreat before and might have been anxious about what they were getting into, this music was a way of taking the fear out of the moment of arrival. It also made it possible for people to sit together in a room without having to introduce themselves and make small talk and yet not seem rude. The retreat, after all, is not a social occasion. We have not come primarily to make friends or pass the time in conversation. The music gives us permission to sit together and to prepare to spend time together without the usual cultural formalities.

I am not convinced of the benefit of playing music at other times, such as meals (in the way texts are read in monastic refectories) or during recreation periods. The problem is that music can be an even more powerful carrier of feelings than words, and whoever chooses what is to be played is almost making a speech to a captive audience.

Of course, music can play a part in a religious retreat when it forms part of the worship. We are psychologically and spiritually prepared for these intervals, and they are less likely to interfere with the routine of our personal work—nor are we obliged to attend them. The kind of hymns or chants repeated day by day in religious houses can be valuable in preparing us at the beginning of the day to enter into the mood. And as the last thing at night, they can help us put aside the thoughts and feelings evoked in our exercises and prepare for sleep.

People who are particularly sensitive to music have told me that they can sometimes identify pieces of music or even write one of their own that can sum up the character of a retreat and act as a way of invoking its spirit for later reflection.

GUIDANCE, INSPIRATION, OR CREATIVITY

IN HIS SPIRITUAL EXERCISES, IGNATIUS LOYOLA PRESENTS A WAY FOR MAKING DECISIONS DURING A RETREAT. THE RETREAT AS A WHOLE IS A TIME WHEN WE FOCUS ON AND SEEK TO DEEPEN OUR RELATIONSHIP WITH GOD AND DISCOVER A DEEPER PURPOSE IN LIFE. IT IS QUITE USUAL, THEREFORE, FOR THOSE ON RETREAT TO FEEL MOVED OR INSPIRED TO MODIFY THEIR LIFE. AS A GENERAL RULE, WE SHOULD BE CAREFUL NOT TO MAKE MAJOR DECISIONS DURING OR IMMEDIATELY AFTER A RETREAT, BECAUSE WE SHOULD RECOGNIZE THAT THE EXPERIENCES AND INSIGHTS WE RECEIVED THEN NEED TIME TO BE INTEGRATED INTO OUR ORDINARY LIVES. A VACATION IS NOT USUALLY AN INSIGHT INTO HOW LIFE MIGHT BE; IT IS A WAY OF HELPING US RETURN TO FACE THE CHALLENGES OF WORK AND RELATIONSHIPS.

The retreat is best thought of as a school for the spirit. It is a time when we have the future and its many possibilities in mind but have to concentrate on the assignments of the moment. Some of us clearly see what we are intended for; others need to balance and consider many factors before making something like a career or educational choice; and still others need to accept that they may only discover their destiny later in life or in quite different circumstances.

Ignatius first states that any matter for decision-making needs to be either good in itself or morally indifferent. Secondly, he distinguishes between permanent decisions and those that could be changed later. We cannot pretend that our enthusiasm for spirituality or self-knowledge exempts us from accepted standards of behavior or gives us liberty to change permanent decisions made earlier. It may be that the most we can hope for is guidance on how to live best in the circumstances in which we find ourselves.

Here are Ignatius's steps toward making a good and sound decision:

1 ••• I bring to mind the matter about which I want to make the decision.

2 ••• I recall the deeper purpose for which I exist: the service of God and of my fellow creatures, and the stewardship of the earth.

3 ••• I compose myself, trying to be like a balance at rest, neither inclined one way nor the other, but ready and willing to move in the direction I perceive to be in accordance with my deeper purpose.

4 ••• I pray that God will put into my mind what I ought to do and move my will to fulfill it.

5 ••• I use my reason and intellect to consider the advantages and disadvantages of acting in this way or that.

6 ••• Having considered the possibilities from every point of view, including how my choice will affect others, I step back to see in which direction my reason—not my emotions—are inclining me.

7 ••• I turn again to prayer, asking that the choice that seems appropriate now will be confirmed in my daily life.

SHARING RETREATS WITH OTHERS

WHENEVER I HEAR THE TERM "SPIRITUAL DIRECTION," I HAVE A PICTURE OF AN ELDERLY ASCETIC (ALWAYS A MAN) IN DARK CLOTHES SITTING IN A CANDLE-LIT ROOM DICTATING STRICT INSTRUCTIONS TO A PIOUS AND RATHER ARISTOCRATIC LADY IN AN OLD-FASHIONED COSTUME WHO IS MAKING NOTES IN A LITTLE BOOK WITH A SILVER PENCIL. IT IS CALLED DIRECTION, BUT WOULD BE BETTER THOUGHT OF AS FOCUSED SPIRITUAL "FRIENDSHIP" OR "CONVERSATION." THE EXPERIENCE OF THE DIVINE IS NOT SOMETHING WE CAN KEEP TO OURSELVES; WE FEEL IMPELLED TO SHARE IT WITH OTHERS AND TO ENCOURAGE THEM TO OPEN THEIR OWN LIVES TO ITS REALITY. FURTHERMORE, WE ARE ENTITLED TO COMPANIONSHIP ALONG THE WAY. THE IDEA OF GUIDING OTHERS IS PART OF THE VERY NATURE OF THE RETREAT.

We all know how inspiring it can be to hear about someone's travels, and the more so if their experiences are presented in an imaginative way. There's nothing very exciting about a list of places visited; what we want to hear about instead are stories of human interest. It is always stimulating to see or hear of creative responses to places visited, such as sketches and journal entries, rather than just be shown mere records, such as most photographs and commercial souvenirs are. A creative response reveals to us how the traveler has actually *seen* and not just looked at a foreign place, in John Ruskin's sense mentioned earlier.

Sharing our spiritual memories and experiences can be a deeply inspiring exercise, if done with another individual or in a small group. When doing so, though, it is advisable to establish some boundaries at the outset:

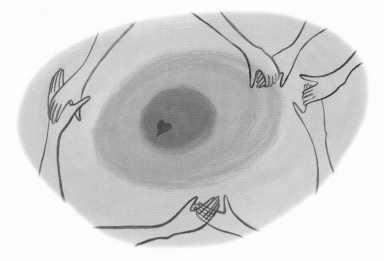

••• At the formative stage, there need to be some criteria established—is it a women's group, a student group, etc. (bearing in mind, of course, that the spirit does not discriminate).

••• Agree that everything shared is confidential to the group.

••• Listen to each other's stories receptively and without interruption.

••• Ask questions for clarification and comparison, but accept that experiences differ.

••• Decide how often and for what length of time you are going to meet—an hour or ninety minutes, depending on how many of you there are, is about right. Also, it is very important to decide how many times you are going to meet—half a dozen is about right to begin with. You can always agree to an extension, but in open-ended groups, other dynamics develop that can become distracting.

••• Lastly, members of the group should make a commitment to attend all the meetings, unless there is a serious reason why they need to be elsewhere.

LEADING
A RETREAT

THROUGHOUT THIS BOOK, I HAVE STRESSED THAT SPIRITUAL GUIDES EMERGE IN COMMUNITIES. THEY ARE NOT THE PRODUCT OF TRAINING COURSES OR THE HOLDERS OF QUALIFICATIONS; INSTEAD, THEY ARE DISCOVERED AND OFTEN RELUCTANTLY RECOGNIZED BY THEIR FELLOW PILGRIMS. THE POINT IS NOT THAT TRAINING IN PARTICULAR SCHOOLS OR METHODS IS INAPPROPRIATE, BUT RATHER THAT IT IS ONLY SUPPLEMENTARY TO RECEPTION OF THE GUIDE BY THE COMMUNITY. SUCH SCHOOLS ARE ALSO VALUABLE FOR THOSE WHO FEEL CALLED TO THIS KIND OF WORK BUT ARE UNSURE OF WHAT IT INVOLVES OR HOW TO STRUCTURE THE PROCESS.

If you have been in a sharing group, you may have become aware that one of you seems to have the particular qualities you would hope for in a "soul friend." It may be that you are the one able to gently share this awareness with them and to encourage them when they no doubt recoil from the very suggestion. Indeed, you may be unfortunate enough to be the one being told!

The most appropriate way to test your vocation to spiritual guidance is to ask other members of the group individually and confidentially if they could imagine you in such a role. If they could, perhaps they might recommend contacts or acquaintances to form a new group in which you would be the facilitator. You would not claim to be a leader but just offer your services as someone who had been in a sharing group before and so was in a position to keep it softly on course. Maybe the individuals who had recognized your gift, or others from the original group, might be prepared to meet with you to support you in the work and offer some kind of sponsorship.

Anyone offering guidance to others should have supervision from another experienced individual or group to whom they should consider themselves accountable. It is important to tell those being guided of this arrangement and, again, to guarantee their confidentiality.

The one who leads a spiritual retreat knows that he or she has the most to learn. It should go without saying that no one takes up the calling to give spiritual guidance for personal gain, publicity, or aggrandizement. The sole reason for doing so is to learn from those who ask for your help.

RESOURCES

Further Reading

Baji-Holms, Karin. *101 Vacations to Change Your Life: A Guide to Wellness Centers, Spiritual Retreats, and Spas.* Carol Publishing Group, 1999.

Cooper, David A. *Silence, Simplicity & Solitude: A Complete Guide to Spiritual Retreat.* SkyLight Paths Publishing, 1999.

Cunningham, Annalisa. *Spa Vacations: Your Guide to Healing Centers and Retreats.* Avalon Travel Publishing, 2001.

Cunningham, Annalisa. *Yoga Vacations: A Guide to International Yoga Retreats.* Avalon Travel Publishing, 1999.

Green, Thomas H. *A Vacation with the Lord: A Personal, Directed Retreat Based on the Spiritual Exercises of Saint Ignatius Loyola.* Ignatius Press, 2000.

Griffin, Emilie. *Wilderness Time: A Guide for Spiritual Retreat.* HarperSanFrancisco, 1998.

Housden, Roger. *Retreat: Time Apart for Silence and Solitude.* HarperCollins, 1995.

Ramon, Brother, and Joyce Huggett (foreword). *Seven Days of Solitude: A Guidebook for a Personal Retreat.* Liguori Publications, 2000.

Jones, Timothy K. *A Place for God: A Guide to Spiritual Retreats and Retreat Centers.* Image, 2000.

Kelly, Jack, and Marcia Kelly. *Sanctuaries: The Complete United States: A Guide to Lodgings in Monasteries, Abbeys, and Retreats.* Bell Tower, 1996.

Kundtz, David. *Quiet Mind: One-Minute Retreats from a Busy World.* Conari Press, 2003.

Lederman, Ellen. *Vacations That Can Change Your Life: Adventures, Retreats, and Workshops for the Mind, Body, and Spirit.* Sourcebooks Trade, 1998.

Mille, Jenifer. *Healing Centers & Retreats: Healthy Getaways for Every Body and Budget.* Avalon Travel Publishing, 1998.

Ocko, Stephanie. *Spiritual Adventures: A Traveler's Guide to Extraordinary Vacations.* Citadel Press, 2003.

INDEX